METROPOLIS

a film by

Fritz Lang 1890-

Simon and Schuster, New York

CONTENTS

A NOTE ON THIS EDITION

Since the original screenplay for the film of *Metropolis* was unobtainable, the version published here has been built up from a shot-by-shot viewing of the version of the film seen in Britain and the United States, with a transcript of the English language titles. Extracts from the English translation of the original novel *Metropolis* by Thea von Harbou, printed in italics in the text, have been added to amplify the text and introduce something of the flavour of the original into the script.

ACKNOWLEDGEMENTS

Acknowledgements and thanks are due to the National Film Archive for providing a print of the film.

The introductory piece by Paul M. Jensen is taken from his book *The Cinema of Fritz Lang,* in the International Film Guide Series, published by A. S. Barnes & Co., New York and A. Zwemmer Limited, London.

The piece by Siegfried Kracauer is taken from his book *From Caligari to Hitler,* published by Dennis Dobson, Ltd., London, and the Princeton University Press.

METROPOLIS: THE FILM AND THE BOOK

by

Paul M. Jensen

Despite UFA's large investment of time and money, Lang's *Nibelungen* films proved successful enough for the studio to give the director *carte blanche* on his next project. Work began in March 1925, and was not concluded until October of the following year. Three hundred and ten days and sixty nights were spent exposing nearly two million feet of negative, while a total of over thirty-six thousand men, women and children were eventually used in front of the cameras. With more than one and a half million marks paid out in salaries alone, the film rapidly became UFA's most expensive picture to date. Even before filming ended, the company's resources were so exhausted that a four million dollar loan from two American studios, Famous Players and Metro-Goldwyn, was needed to avert financial disaster. By the time the production was finished, the company owed more than forty million marks to the Deutsche Bank (its main backer) and to several other concerns.

Because of this, the immediate financial future of UFA depended upon *Metropolis,* the "costliest and most ambitious picture ever screened in Europe."* The film was premièred on January 10, 1927 at the UFA Palace, in Berlin, before an enormous audience which included Cabinet officers, members of the diplomatic corps, and the city's major social, artistic, and literary figures. Critically, however, *Metropolis* did not meet expectations; its visual and technical qualities were praised, but the simplistic and sentimental social content was harshly condemned. Though it attracted large audiences (ten thousand people were reported waiting outside the Rialto Theatre at its American opening), the movie still could not recover its tremendous investment and save UFA.

When the practically bankrupt company was refused a state subsidy, it passed into the hands of Alfred Hugenberg, a powerful newspaper publisher who also owned the country largest non-official news agency. Backed by the Nationalist Party, Hugenberg took complete control of UFA in April 1927, when he was able to

---

* '*Metropolis* Film Seen', *The New York Times* (March 6, 1927).

seat nineteen members on the Executive Committee of twenty-seven. His interest in the 135 theatres and two giant studios of Germany's largest film company was supposedly strictly personal. As one-man "dictator" of films, he could determine the political character of his own productions and specify which foreign pictures would be shown in UFA houses. It appears, however, that the company's practical distress forced him to postpone spreading reactionary propaganda until its finances were stabilised.

The motion picture that caused the downfall of the "old" UFA was first conceived in 1924. With *Siegfrieds Tod* enjoying successful runs in London and Paris, Lang visited America to study the local movie industry. He arrived from Hamburg in October 1924, accompanied by producer Erich Pommer, Felix Kallmann (President of UFA), and Frederick Wynne-Jones (the company's American representative). During their seven-week stay they visited nearly all the studios and met with many film-makers, including Ernst Lubitsch. It is said that while looking at the New York skyline from the deck of his ship, Lang thought of setting a film in such a city far in the future. He discussed this idea with his wife, Thea von Harbou, and she wrote a novel based on it, which the two then converted into a scenario.

In the year 2000, Freder, the son of the Master of Metropolis, rebels against the way his half of the city—the idle "aristocracy"—has dehumanised the labourers. Limited to lives of hard and lengthy work, the latter live underground, below the halls where the machines are located. Potential rebellion has been prevented by Maria, who urges her companions to await the arrival of a mediator who will unite the city. Freder is that saviour, but he is hindered by his father, who orders a robot that exactly duplicates Maria to spread dissatisfaction among the workers. The plan succeeds and a mob smashes the machines, thus causing their own homes to be flooded. Thinking that they have drowned their children, the workers attack the robot and burn "her". Meanwhile, Freder and the real Maria have rescued the children. Suddenly Rotwang, a scientist who built the robot, chases the girl on to the cathedral roof. Freder follows, and in the ensuing struggle Rotwang loses his balance and falls to his death. Seeing his son's danger, Joh Fredersen relents and agrees to shake hands with a representative of the workers.

6

In 1928, Fritz Lang and Thea von Harbou were charged with plagiarism when a certain Frau Debeke declared that she had sent Pommer and Lang a scenario containing every element in *Metropolis,* and that it was returned to her with the comment that it would not be used. "When Frau Debeke returned to Berlin, after a long absence, she was surprised to find the film *Metropolis* advertised."* The amount of truth in this accusation is unknown, but whoever did originate the story was not being entirely original. No doubt *R.U.R.,* Karel Capek's play about mechanical workers, and the Russian silent film *Aelita* (1924) affected the concept, and H. G. Wells found "decaying fragments of my own juvenile work of thirty years ago, *The Sleeper Wakes,* floating about in it." Wells's *The Time Machine* contains a very similar social division.

Metropolis was re-edited for its 1927 American release by Channing Pollock (a playwright), Julian Johnson, and Edward Adams; about seven reels were cut from the original seventeen. This condensed version, lacking almost half the intended footage, is still the only one available. The novel has recently been published in translation, however, so the abbreviated picture can now be compared with its original plot. This makes it clear that while *Metropolis* was naïve and silly to start with, the elimination of many scenes and the re-writing of some titles have excessively confused certain motivations and characters. For example, what happens to Josaphat, the secretary who is kept from suicide, or to the worker whose place Freder takes when he visits the cavern of machines? Both characters are introduced in the prints available, then abruptly disappear.

More important to the plot is the question of why Joh Fredersen, Freder's father and the Master of Metropolis, wants to have the workers lose confidence in Maria. She preaches patience and peace to the rebellious workers, and this would seem to be to Joh's advantage. But instead of acting logically, Joh sends the robot Maria to impel the workers to criminal acts, and when they revolt he orders his foreman to throw open the doors, thus allowing them to destroy the machines, flood their homes, and perhaps drown their forgotten children. A title says that he is "looking for an excuse to use violence against the workers," but since his method cripples the city's

---

* ' Claims *Metropolis* Play', *The New York Times* (December 23, 1928).

ability to function, he is also working against his own interests and those of the upper classes he represents. This problem originated in Mrs. Lang's novel, though, and was not caused later by the film's editors.

With the false Maria out on her mission, the real one is imprisoned by the scientist-mystic Rotwang. In the American version she is suddenly shown to be free, and her escape is never explained. Since Rotwang is presented as a villain, we are also bothered by seeing him speak kindly to Maria in her "cell". He even seems to offer his hand in friendship, and later, when she is free, he tells her, "If the mob sees you they will kill you for having tricked them." This seems a well-intentioned warning, but Maria suddenly turns and flees from him; then he, surprisingly, chases her on to the cathedral roof and fights with Freder. Such behaviour is inexplicable in the context of the titles and scenes we have been shown, but the novel reveals how re-editing eliminated Rotwang's motivation and destroyed the picture's continuity.

The key change was the removal of all mention of the woman Hel, who had died before the start of the story. Though loved by Rotwang, she had not been able to resist Joh Fredersen and had gone away with him. She died giving birth to Freder, but it was really Joh's excessively strong love and her own guilt at ruining Rotwang's life that killed her. The resulting antagonism between the two men gives Joh's dependence on Rotwang for advice and inventions an edge of irony that the film lacks.

While talking with the imprisoned Maria, Rotwang declares, "Joh Fredersen took the woman from me. He made me evil . . . but I will defy the Will which is above you and me. I will open the door for you . . . If you give me your hands I will go with you into the City of the Dead, so that you can warn your brothers, so that you can unmask your stolen ego." This dialogue does not appear in present prints of *Metropolis*, though part of the scene is included without titles.

At this point in the novel Joh enters and attacks Rotwang, and during the struggle Maria escapes. When Rotwang regains consciousness he thinks he is dead, and so goes in search of Hel. He mistakes Maria for his love, and when she flees to the cathedral he chases after her uncomprehendingly. As the sequences leading up to this final encounter are now missing from the film, the characters'

8

actions seem strange, to say the least. It is to Rudolf Klein-Rogge's credit that even though needed scenes have been excised and new titles added, a viewer still senses more to Rotwang's character than is actually shown; suspicions of sympathy are aroused, and are not entirely overshadowed by the mad-scientist stereotype being forced on him.

A foot race which Freder ran at the start of the film was also removed, though photos of the vast stadium still exist. Other missing scenes are those devoted to Yoshiwara, a shell-shaped auditorium where a crowd shares a common narcotic delusion in which one of them becomes "the embodied conception of the intoxication of them all . . . Each of the thousands of others in ecstasy lives the thousandfold ecstasy which embodies itself in him." It is here that the freed worker ends up, and where he goes mad at the new sensation.

Randolph Bartlett, writing in *The New York Times,* tried to defend this technique of re-editing. The Germans, he said, have either a "lack of interest in dramatic verity or an astonishing ineptitude. Motives were absent . . . or were extremely naive," and so the importers decided to improve the narrative technique. The case of Freder's mother, however, presented another problem. According to Bartlett, one shot showed:

> a very beautiful statue of a woman's head, and on the base was her name—and that name was "Hel". Now, the German word for "hell" is "hoelle" so they were quiet [*sic*] innocent of the fact that this name would create a guffaw in an English speaking country. So it was necessary to cut this beautiful bit out of the picture, and a certain motive which it represented had to be replaced by another.*

So, haunted by fears of Hel, the editors snipped out all references to this major plot thread. Unfortunately, they failed to provide the promised replacement and simply left actions unexplained. The editors were trying "to bring out the real thought that was manifestly back of the production, and which the Germans had simply 'muffed'," said Bartlett. "I am willing to wager that *Metropolis,* as it is seen at the Rialto now, is nearer Fritz Lang's idea than the

---

* Bartlett, Randolph. 'German Film Revision Upheld as Needed Here', *The New York Times* (March 13, 1927).

version he himself released in Germany . . . When we add to this the fact that American audiences require fare far different from that of the European, we multiply the necessity for adaptation." On the other hand, after seeing what he calls the "mutilated surrogate" of his film, Lang supposedly vowed never to direct in the United States.

Though both film and book are philosophically muddled, it is still possible to isolate certain themes. For example, the duality of human nature that fascinates Lang is here in abundance. The split in each individual between the mental and the physical has evolved, by the year 2000, into a social division. One group of people retains only the brain, while another uses only muscle. These extremes are geographically and pictorially contrasted, with the underground workers marching slowly in tight formation while the rulers cavort freely in pleasure gardens on the surface. Yet the two types are also "brothers", and complementary parts of a single organism.

Another dichotomy is that of a female's dual natures, schematically divided into the characters played by Brigitte Helm. The real Maria embodies purity and virginity, while her mechanical double is an evil, seductive harlot; at the same time, these two also contrast humanity with its opposite, the machine. This reflects the division between the free rulers and the machine-like workers they control. Eventually, the suppressed humanity of the latter group breaks free of its regular formations, and a mob results which destroys ordered patterns and instead acts according to emotional impulse.

When Freder becomes a mediator, he begins to function as a typical Lang hero: he is an outsider separate from and caught between the two halves of his society. Lang represents this quite literally by having the character descend into the area of the machines, which is situated above the workers' homes and below the surface city. Now on his own, Freder is involved in a seemingly impossible struggle; he is opposed on all sides by both good and evil, friend and foe. His father tries to limit his investigations, the workers resentfully turn on him when they find out who he is, the secretary whose life he saved betrays him (in the novel), and even Maria seems for a time to have deserted him. With no one to trust, he works alone against both groups in order to synthesise them.

According to Maria the heart must mediate between the hand

and the mind, so Freder represents the heart (hence, also the emotions) and his humanity avoids the taint of mechanisation. This may explain, though never justify, the curious acting of Gustav Fröhlich in the role. Freder is all impulse, and the tendency to incline his head forward and charge blindly from place to place is a misguided attempt to illustrate this characteristic.

Besides advocating emotions as a solution to the lack of communication between leaders and labour, Fritz Lang also supports this approach because it allows humanity to triumph over machines. This simplification of a highly complex problem is difficult to take seriously, and therefore one of the film's major flaws. It can only be attributed to the director's romantic-expressionistic faith in victory through love (as seen in the ending of *Der müde Tod*). Yet Lang contradicts himself, for while favouring the emotions he also sees them as impulsively producing the weaknesses and violence which cause a character's destruction (as in the case of the murderer in *M* and the lynch mob in *Fury*.) Thus a person who is calm and pleasant on the surface may contain within him unknown depths of violence, and a man may one day find these forces fighting to take command. When primitive emotions control many people at the same time, the result is a mob. In such a case, a whole city or society may be said to suffer a revolt from beneath its surface, as witness many of the race riots in America. In *Metropolis,* this is made literal by placing the city of the rebelling workers deep within the earth. The implacable flood they cause is a striking visual parallel to the escape of these pent-up emotions, and here Lang's classical attitude toward the passions unwittingly conflicts with his romanticism and makes the blind blundering of Freder seem a false ideal, indeed.

Lang often creates a master-opponent such as Dr. Mabuse to embody all the forces against a hero, and Joh Fredersen is assigned that function here. From his tower office, above the city and distant from others, he controls his world with the "infallible certainty of a healthy machine." He lives by his own laws and imposes his will on all. However, it is never made clear what prompts such an omnipotent force to create a revolt among the workers. If there is a reason, it is not supplied in the work itself; if it is an arbitrary action, Fredersen does not deserve the position and respect he is accorded. His authority is also weakened by his dependence on Rotwang for aid.

Metropolis contains an abundance of direct, unsubtle religious references. Freder, the only son of Joh (Jehovah), is destined to redeem the common people and unite the divided world. Maria (Mary) combines the function of prophet, predicting the arrival of the messiah-mediator, with elements of both the Virgin Mary (who "creates" him) and the prostitute one. Freder refers to everyone else as his brother, and (in the novel) addresses a statue of the Virgin as "Mother". Labouring with extended arms at the clock-machine, he prays to his Father for deliverance; he has taken upon himself the weight of suffering imposed on the workers, as well as the guilt of the rulers who impose it.

The Joh-Jehovah parallel notwithstanding, the closest Lang has come to presenting a God is in the figure of Death in *Der müde Tod*. That character of course is not defeated at the end, but Lang's more secular menaces such as the criminal organisation heads can usually be overcome. Joh Fredersen is a combination of both types of antagonist, though instead of merging into a single complex figure they tend to alternate from scene to scene.

The defeat of an Unconquerable Menace is a convention of melodrama, meant to offer the viewer a limited feeling of security. The question is, how acceptable within its own framework is the conclusion of each particular plot? The ending of *Metropolis* is not prepared for and so fails to satisfy. It is one thing to destroy a threat, and quite another for that threat to see the light and to reform. Joh's "conversion" from his earlier views completely disregards the suggestions of infallibility already established. On the other hand, Siegfried Kracauer's conclusion that "the industrialist acknowledges the heart for the purpose of manipulating it" is a delusion, for the novel assures us (though it is hard to accept) that Fredersen's heart really is "utterly redeemed."

The formalised actions of the workers are far more successful than the rulers' now comic decadence, which includes an extraneous, seductive dance by the female robot. Young Brigitte Helm, in her first screen appearance, is impressive as both the mechanical vamp and the heroine with the innocent Gish-Pickford look, while Gustav Fröhlich fails as the effusive Freder. In contrast, Alfred Abel keeps a tight rein on Joh Fredersen's restraint and dignity, even in his final moments of kneeling remorse. In fact, the viewer sympathises more with the rational father than with the simple-minded overly-emotional son. Commanding the appeal of Shaw's industrialist in *Major Barbara,* he is a kind of ultimate Undershaft.

Lang's hero struggles against his entire environment, including everything human (a mob, Fredersen) and inanimate (the flood, a series of opening and closing doors that lures him through several rooms in Rotwang's house). Everything is a threat, even a seemingly innocent object. This feeling is best communicated during Maria's panic-stricken flight through the underground tunnels, as she struggles to free herself from the beam of light that thrusts her forward. This exciting and skilful sequence uses the moving camera, and light and darkness, to create an implacable Unknown from which there is no escape. This is the atmosphere of Lang's world, with an intangible threat existing nowhere but felt everywhere.

Despite such occasional atmospheric success, *Metropolis* is simply a compendium of Lang's themes with none sufficiently dramatised to make it meaningful. There is mob violence, seduction, insanity, duality of good and evil, the innocent hero, the threatening environment, the master-mind, opposing social forces, the virtues of love, and even an attempt at science-mysticism-religion. But it is not for any of these that the film will be remembered.

Aside from the atmosphere mentioned above, the chief merit of *Metropolis* is its visual style. Most individual shots are carefully composed, with the emphasis on a balanced arrangement of objects within the frame. The organisation of shapes is formalised, but seldom as static as the picture's detractors claim. Many scenes require movement for their effects, such as when the edge of the flood approaches the fleeing children; in another case, only a few workers at the Tower of Babel are standing in the foreground until a shift in position reveals thousands in the distance.

The settings, particularly the workers' homes, are stylised into mere forms with black rectangles for windows. A number of these were models, which were combined with live actors through the Schüfftan process. Invented by photographer Eugene Schüfftan, it used a camera with two lenses which focused two separate images onto a single strip of film; this allowed actors and models to be recorded together without resorting to double exposure or laboratory work. The designs are expressionistic; but the architect in

Lang rebelled against the surface distortion and linear anarchy of *Caligari's* use of the style. Instead, his settings are solid and substantial, extending in more than two dimensions. Their design is regular, controlled and organised, dwelling on simplicity rather than clutter.

The moving camera is used sparingly, with the aim of heightening emotional empathy in certain scenes of excitement. A swinging camera, similar in effect to today's zoom lens, is used when Freder is stunned by the first explosion, later when he faints at seeing Maria with his father, and finally when he collapses on a stairway during the final holocaust. The major tracking shot occurs when we follow Maria through the catacombs, as Rotwang forces her on with his flashlight.

A painter's eye for composition and staging is again revealed in Lang's direction. Any selection of the best examples tends to be determined by memory and subjective inclination, but particularly effective are the bearing of injured workers in silhouette past Freder, the shots of children running along the street with the water's edge flowing a few seconds behind them, and the tent of electricity surrounding the robot during the creation scene. Only in *Die Nibelungen,* and to a lesser extent in *Der müde Tod,* did Lang allow his painter's eye and architect's pen to create as much excitement; in his other films he adapted himself to varying degrees of realism. But the romantic legends of *Siegfrieds Tod* and *Kriemhilds Rache* perfectly blend with a classical form, while *Metropolis* is unwisely treated as though it too were another romantic legend. Actually, the basic conceptions of the city and of the themes are intellectual, and so conflict with the childish sentimentality of the plotting, motivations, and feelings. The content of *Metropolis* fails to live up to its visual treatment, but the film is still a treat to the eye.

INDUSTRIALISM AND TOTALITARIANISM

by

Siegfried Kracauer

The following piece from Siegfried Kracauer's book From Caligari
to Hitler *is taken from the section dealing with the films made in
Germany in the period after the stabilization of the mark in 1924.
These are divided by Kracauer into three categories, the first of
which 'simply testifies to the existence of a state of paralysis. The
second group sheds light on the tendencies and notions that are
paralyzed. The third reveals the inner workings of the paralyzed
collective soul.'* Metropolis *is placed by Kracauer in the second
category, which, he says, also includes two groups of films, the
'street' films, dealing with the theme of the street and prostitution,
and the 'youth' films—films featuring children or adolescents. Both
of these categories deal with the theme of rebellion against the
established authority, while the youth films, paradoxically 'affirm
fixation to authoritarian behaviour precisely by stressing rebellion
against it'.*

One film was more explicit than all others: *Metropolis*. In it
the paralyzed collective mind seemed to be talking with unusual
clarity in its sleep. This is more than a metaphor: owing to a for-
tunate combination of receptivity and confusion, Lang's script
writer, Thea von Harbou, was not only sensitive to all under-
currents of the time, but indiscriminately passed on whatever
happened to haunt her imagination. *Metropolis* was rich in subterranean content that, like contraband, had crossed the borders of
consciousness without being questioned.

Freder, son of the mammoth industrialist who controls the whole
of Metropolis, is true to type: he rebels against his father and joins
the workers in the lower city. There he immediately becomes a
devotee of Maria, the great comforter of the oppressed. A saint
rather than a socialist agitator, this young girl delivers a speech
to the workers in which she declares that they can be redeemed only

if the heart mediates between hand and brain. And she exhorts her listeners to be patient: soon the mediator will come. The industrialist, having secretly attended this meeting, deems the interference of the heart so dangerous that he entrusts an inventor with the creation of a robot looking exactly like Maria. This robot-Maria is to incite riots and furnish the industrialist with a pretext to crush the workers' rebellious spirit. He is not the first German screen tyrant to use such methods; Homunculus had introduced them much earlier. Stirred by the robot, the workers destroy their torturers, the machines, and release flood waters which then threaten to drown their own children. If it were not for Freder and the genuine Maria, who intervene at the last moment, all would be doomed. Of course, this elemental outburst has by far surpassed the petty little uprising for which the industrialist arranged. In the final scene, he is shown standing between Freder and Maria, and the workers approach, led by their foreman. Upon Freder's suggestion, his father shakes hands with the foreman, and Maria happily consecrates this symbolic alliance between labor and capital.

On the surface, it seems that Freder has converted his father; in reality, the industrialist has outwitted his son. The concession he makes amounts to a policy of appeasement that not only prevents the workers from winning their cause, but enables him to tighten his grip on them. His robot stratagem was a blunder inasmuch as it rested upon insufficient knowledge of the mentality of the masses. By yielding to Freder, the industrialist achieves intimate contact with the workers, and thus is in a position to influence their mentality. He allows the heart to speak—a heart accessible to his insinuations.

In fact, Maria's demand that the heart mediate between hand and brain could well have been formulated by Goebbels. He, too, appealed to the heart—in the interest of totalitarian propaganda. At the Nuremberg Party Convention of 1934, he praised the "art" of propaganda as follows: "May the shining flame of our enthusiasm never be extinguished. This flame alone gives light and warmth to the creative art of modern political propaganda. Rising from the depths of the people, this art must always descend back to it and find its power there. Power based on guns may be a good thing; it is, however, better and more gratifying to win the heart

16

of a people and to keep it." The pictorial structure of the final scene confirms the analogy between the industrialist and Goebbels. If in this scene the heart really triumphed over tyrannical power, its triumph would dispose of the all-devouring decorative scheme that in the rest of *Metropolis* marks the industrialist's claim to omnipotence. Artist that he was, Lang could not possibly overlook the antagonism between the breakthrough of intrinsic human emotions and his ornamental patterns. Nevertheless, he maintains these patterns up to the very end : the workers advance in the form of a wedge-shaped, strictly symmetrical procession which points towards the industrialist standing on the portal steps of the cathedral. The whole composition denotes that the industrialist acknowledges the heart for the purpose of manipulating it ; that he does not give up his power, but will expand it over a realm not yet annexed—the realm of the collective soul. Freder's rebellion results in the establishment of totalitarian authority, and he considers this result a victory.

Freder's pertinent reaction corroborates what has been said about the way in which the street films as well as the youth films anticipate the change of the "system". Now it can no longer be doubted that the "new order" both series foreshadow is expected to feed upon that love with which Asta Nielsen's prostitute* overflows, and to substitute totalitarian discipline for the obsolete mechanical one. In the case of *Metropolis,* Goebbels' own words bear out the conclusions drawn from this film. Lang relates that immediately after Hitler's rise to power Goebbels sent for him : ". . . he told me that, many years before, he and the Führer had seen my picture *Metropolis* in a small town, and Hitler had said at that time that he wanted me to make the Nazi pictures."**

---

* In Bruno Rahn's *Dirnentragödie (Tragedy of the Street,* 1927).
** "Fritz Lang", *New York World Telegram* (June 11, 1941).

CREDITS:

Screenplay by	Fritz Lang and Thea von Harbou
From the novel by	Thea von Harbou
Directed by	Fritz Lang
Photography	Karl Freund, Günther Rittau
Art directors	Otto Hunte, Erich Kettelhut, Karl Volbrecht
Sculpture	Walter Schultze-Mittendorf
Costumes	Aenne Willkomm
Producer	Erich Pommer
Production company	UFA

CAST:

Alfred Abel	John Fredersen
Gustav Fröhlich	Freder
Brigitte Helm	Maria/the robot
Rudolf Klein-Rogge	Rotwang
Fritz Rasp	Slim
Theodor Loos	Joseph
Erwin Biswanger	Georg (No. 11811)
Heinrich George	Grot, the foreman

with
Fritz Alberti, Grete Berger, Olly Böheim, Max Dietze, Ellen Frey, Beatrice Garga, Heinrich Gotho, Lisa Gray, Anny Hintze, Georg John, Walter Kuhle, Margarete Lanner, Rose Lichtenstein, Helen von Münchhofen, Hanns Leo Reich, Arthur Reinhard, Olaf Storm, Erwin Vater, Helene Weigel, Hilde Woitscheff.

METROPOLIS

*When the sun sank at the back of Metropolis, the houses
turned to mountains and the streets to valleys, and a stream
of light, which seemed to crackle with coldness, broke forth
from all the windows.*

A series of diagonal lines appearing from opposite sides of the
screen form the opening title: METROPOLIS. Light shines
through the letters in prismatic patterns, while the towers and
tenements of the city appear in iris behind. Shadows move across
the scene as we dissolve to a series of shots of the great machines
of Metropolis:

Gigantic pyramidal pistons moving slowly up and down./Wheels
turning./Electrical insulators./Rods and gleaming shafts./Cams
and winding gear./The slow-moving cogs of a great machine./The
valve gear of a vast steam chest, moving slowly to and fro./More
cogs moving slowly./Cogs and wheels superimposed. Dissolve.

*On the enormous face of the clock in the New Tower of Babel
—the machine centre of Metropolis—the seconds ticked off,
continuous in their coming as in their going.*

The clock is divided into ten segments only; the two main hands
are almost in the vertical position, while the second hand sweeps
jerkily round.

Another shot of pistons, gears and cable drums superimposed,
turning and reciprocating.

On the clock, the second hand reaches the vertical position.

Amid the cliff-like office blocks and factories of the city, white
steam blasts from a siren.

*Metropolis raised her voice. The machines of Metropolis
roared; they wanted to be fed.*

Title: The day shift.

A great steel grille bars the passage into the machine rooms of
Metropolis. A column of ingoing workers stand in back view on the
right, while the outgoing shift faces us through the grille. The
grille slowly rises.

Then the living food came pushing along in masses . . . Men,

men, men—all in the same uniform, from throat to ankle in dark blue linen, bare feet in the same hard shoes, hair tightly pressed down by the same black caps.

We look down the cavernous corridor. A light goes on in the central pillar of the gateway and the day-shift files in at a rapid shambling walk, while the out-going shift comes slowly out at half the speed.

And they all had the same faces. And they all seemed one thousand years old . . . They planted their feet forward but they did not walk. The open gates of the New Tower of Babel, the machine centre of Metropolis, threw up the masses as it gulped them down.

Seen in reverse shot, the two shifts file past one another.

Then the blasting siren is seen again from below.

The Pater Noster—the never-stop passenger lift which, like a series of never ceasing well-buckets, trans-sected the New Tower of Babel—gathered men up and poured them out again.

We are looking down towards one of the cages of the passenger lift; the ingoing men appear at the bottom of frame and file towards it, six abreast . . .

While in the corridor, the two shifts are still filing past one another. At the lift, the final row of six men crowd in, in an orderly fashion. A gate rises to waist height in front of them; the operator turns a wheel and the lift sinks slowly down, accompanied by the camera.

TITLE: THE WORKERS' CITY FAR BELOW THE SURFACE OF THE EARTH.

The camera continues to move with the lift, down the gloomy shaft. It reaches the bottom and we look out over the bent heads of the workers to the tall tenement blocks of the workers' city, rising beneath a vast ceiling.

Seen from outside, the cage comes to a halt at the bottom of the shaft. The gate is lowered and the workers plod forward in unison, starting at the ground.

Men, men, men—and they all seemed one thousand years old.
They walked with hanging fists, they walked with hanging
heads. No, they planted their feet forward but they did not

walk. . . .

We now see three lift shafts, side by side, a column of workers emerging from each one; the lifts start to rise again in the background.

> *. . .And the horrible sobriety of these houses, in which there lived not men, but numbers, recognisable only by the enormous placards by the house doors.*

A high shot looks down onto a big square in the centre of the workers' city. The tenement blocks rise on either side, light streaming from windows and doorways, while in the centre stands a vast gong on a pedestal with an automatic beater operated by two levers. The columns of workers trudge forward from the bottom of frame, dispersing towards their dwellings in the background. Fade out.

> *The 'Club of the Sons' was, perhaps, one of the most beautiful of Metropolis, and that was not so very remarkable. For fathers, for whom every revolution of a machine-wheel spelt gold, had presented this house to their sons. It was more a district than a house. It embraced theatres, picture-palaces, lecture-rooms and a library . . . race tracks and stadium and the famous 'Eternal Gardens'.*

TITLE: DEEP AS THE WORKMEN'S CITY LAY UNDERGROUND, SO HIGH ABOVE IT TOWERED THE MASTERMAN STADIUM, GIFT OF JOHN MASTERMAN, THE RICHEST MAN IN METROPOLIS.

We see the towering walls of the vast stadium, surmounted by statues of athletes. In the background is a large enclosed arena, while in the foreground, athletes and young men are preparing for a race.

One of the young men, Freder, is chatting animatedly to a companion off-screen. Then he turns towards us and applauds the athletes.

> *He wore, as all the youths in the 'House of the Sons', the white silk, which they wore but once—the soft, supple shoes, with the noiseless soles.*

The young men in white silk stand watching as the athletes assemble for the race.

Freder raises an arm in the air.

And the athletes, all stripped to the waist, crouch on their marks at the start.

Freder sweeps his arm down in the starting signal . . .

And the runners pelt away up the track.

Camera tracks in front of the running athletes . . .

While the young men run across to the other side of the stadium.

There, they run up and stand waiting at the finishing tape. They shout and wave their arms, egging the runners on.

Again we track with the runners. They are all young and healthy, filled with boyish enthusiasm.

At the finish, the bystanders shout and wave as the winner crosses the tape, followed by the other athletes.

TITLE : BUT ATHLETICS WERE NOT THE ONLY DIVERSION OF GILDED YOUTH IN METROPOLIS.

We move to the Eternal Gardens, in the Club of the Sons . . .

> *The milk-coloured glass ceiling above the Eternal Gardens was an opal in the light which bathed it . . .*

. . . Strange convoluted stalactites rise to the ceiling; there are ferns

and greenery on every side. In the centre stands a thin, grey-haired Major-domo, in tail coat and white buttery collar; he claps his hands and a bevy of girls in erotic, sequinned costumes converge on him slowly.

> *With their bewildering costume, their painted faces, and their eyemasks, surmounted by snow-white wigs and fragrant as flowers, they resembled delicate dolls of porcelain and brocade, devised by a master hand, not purchaseable but rather delightful presents.*

We see two of the girls; one of them steps towards the Major-domo, off-screen, while the other shows us her naked back, covered with exotic sequinned designs.

Another girl in a three-cornered hat and a crinoline skirt, her naked breasts covered by a diaphanous shawl, curtseys to the Major-domo off-screen.

Another girl in more contemporary garments, with an elaborate head-dress, curtseys towards camera.

The girls stand clustered round the Major-domo; several of them walk off in the foreground, while he turns to the others beside the convoluted columns behind him.

They were handsome well-trained female servants for whose training more time was requisite than for the development of new species of orchids.

The Major-domo—thin faced, elderly, with glasses, a white lace handkerchief clutched delicately in his hand—turns to the girls off-screen, gesturing and explaining how they should receive their guests.

In response to his gestures, the girl in the three-cornered hat pirouettes daintily, showing us her naked back.

The Major-domo motions her the other way round . . .

And the girl pirouettes once again.

In a high angle long shot a half-naked girl suddenly runs across from the foreground and dodges behind one of the convoluted columns; a youth in white silk—it is Freder—chases after her, but the other girls playfully block his path. A game of hide and seek ensues as Freder chases the girl round and round the columns, gaily shouting and laughing. They finally rush off to the left.

Like a joyously ringing rainbow, peal upon peal of laughter arched itself gaily above the young people.

In another part of the garden, fountains are playing and peacocks strutting about on the lawns. Framed by glittering jets of water, the girl rushes in and hides behind another fountain, while Freder appears in pursuit and looks from side to side.

Water sparkles across the screen as the girl, in a black costume and three-cornered hat, peeps out from behind the fountain and shouts, throwing up her naked arms.

Title : 'Freder!'

Freder whips round at the sound of her voice.

The girl grins and waves from behind the fountain . . .

And Freder starts forward with a gleam in his eye.

The peacocks scatter as he chases her round and round the fountain basin.

She crouches to one side, calling across to him playfully.

Freder, on the opposite side, shouts back with a grin, and darts round the side of the fountain.

Again the two of them dodge to and fro round the basin, the girl showing us her naked back and legs.

Freder is framed by the glittering spray as he calls playfully across to the girl.

Also framed by the water, the girl dances up and down, waving her arms.

Freder dashes through the spray, waving his arms . . .

And they dance around the basin once again.

The girl is seen in profile; she darts away to the left as Freder makes another dive for her.

On the opposite side of the fountain, she dances up and down, egging him on.

Freder splashes water at the girl off-screen.

She screams playfully and runs off.

Freder darts forward at the same time . . .

And the two of them collide in front of the fountain. Freder takes the girl in his arms; she screams and giggles as he leans over her, talking and laughing. Slowly, she puts her arms around his neck.

> *Her gleaming body rose, delicately, from her hips and quivered in the same rhythm as did the man's chest in exhaling his sweet-rising breath.*

They are seen in close-up as Freder leans over her and brings his mouth towards hers.

Suddenly we look towards the ornamental doors leading into the Eternal Gardens. Long-necked cranes teeter to and fro in front of the steps leading up to the doorway. The doors open a fraction.

Just as he is about to kiss the girl, Freder looks up . . .

As the doors swing slowly open to reveal a young woman standing with arms outstretched, a crowd of ragged children behind her. She comes slowly forward across the threshold.

Freder releases the girl, staring towards the doorway; she straightens up, looking round also.

> *Through the door came a procession of children. They were all holding hands. They had dwarves' faces, grey and ancient. They were little ghost-like skeletons, covered with faded rags and smocks. They had colourless hair and colourless eyes. They walked on emaciated bare feet. Noiselessly they followed their leader.*

The young woman, whose name is Maria, advances slowly to the edge of the steps; the children of Metropolis crowd in behind her. A closer shot of Maria, with hazed iris effect, as she walks forward,

her arms round several of the children. They look round in wonder
at the garden, peering and pointing.

> *The laughter ceased, not one of the friends moved. Not one of
> the little, brocaded, bare-limbed women moved hand or foot.
> They stood and looked.*

Freder and the girl stand watching by the fountain, while the other
girls crowd forward anxiously, looking at the spectacle off-screen.

> *The leader was a girl. The austere countenance of the Virgin.
> The sweet countenance of the mother. She held a skinny child
> by each hand. Now she stood still, regarding the young men
> and women one after the other, with the deadly severity of
> purity.*

Maria is seen in iris, simply clad in a dress with a large white collar.
The children crowd round her, looking up at her face as she gazes
intently at the others off-screen.

Freder stands with the girl looking anxiously over his shoulder; she
clutches at him, but he puts out an arm, fending her off, staring
transfixed at Maria.

> *She was quite maid and mistress, inviolability — and was,*

too, graciousness itself, her beautiful brow in the diadem of
goodness; her voice, pity; every word a song.

Still seen in iris, Maria raises her arms; her gaze rests on Freder as
she says:

TITLE: 'LOOK—THESE ARE YOUR BROTHERS.'

Maria calls the children forward, turning from side to side and
pointing to the spectacle in front of them . . .
While the gilded youth of Metropolis stand amid the greenery and
the convoluted columns, all gazing in bewilderment towards the
doorway.
Freder, above all, cannot take his eyes off Maria.
She stands, in close-up, her gaze resting perpetually on him . . .
While he stands gazing back, the girl looking in bewilderment over
his shoulder.

> *Then the servants came, the door-keepers came. Between these*
> *walls of marble and glass, under the opal dome of the Eternal*
> *Gardens, there reigned, for a short time, an unprecedented*
> *confusion of noise, indignation and embarrassment.*

Long shot of the scene in the doorway. Flunkeys in waistcoats stand on either side. The Major-domo bustles forward and scuttles to and fro, interrogating the flunkeys: but they all shrug and wave their arms. He motions to them to throw the children out.

The girl still appeared to be waiting. Nobody dared to touch her, though she stood so defenceless, among the grey infant phantoms.

The children are seen in iris in the doorway, Maria in their centre. One of the flunkeys comes up and addresses her; she starts to move slowly backwards . . .

Seen in close-up as she gazes intensely at Freder.

More flunkeys have appeared at the doorway; Maria calls to the children, turns and ushers them out, driving her flock in front of her. The flunkeys follow behind.

Freder is still transfixed, his hand clutched to his heart. The girl at his side puts her hand on his and speaks soothingly, but he starts forward, pushing her aside.

Meanwhile the doors swing to behind the departing children as the flunkeys follow them out.

Freder steps down from the fountain basin and addresses the Major-domo off-screen.

TITLE: 'WHO WAS THAT?'

Freder stands at the bottom of the steps while the Major-domo comes back through the doors and explains with hopeless gestures:

TITLE: 'JUST THE DAUGHTER OF A WORKER.'

The Major-domo stands watching anxiously as Freder clutches his fists to his chest and, as if in a trance, suddenly walks off.

He felt the soulless glance of the strange, hired person upon his face. He felt himself poor and besmirched. In an ill-temper which rendered him as wretched as though he had poison in his veins, he left the club.

Freder rushes out and goes down some steps in the background, leaving the doors swinging behind him. Fade out.

TITLE: THE GREAT MACHINES, FAR UNDERGROUND, YET HIGH ABOVE THE WORKERS' CITY.

We are looking down into one of the vast machine-rooms of Metropolis. Great girders are supported on concrete piles; near the ceiling vast drums revolve and lights flash, while on either side workers clad in overalls stand at panels, watching dials and throwing switches in rhythmic, mechanical movements. Freder walks forward in the centre of the shot, a tiny white figure, and looks round in wonder at the scene.

A closer shot as he comes round one of the great concrete plinths and looks up in amazement . . .

> *In the middle of the room crouched the Pater Noster machine. It was like Ganesha, the god with the elephant's head. It shone with oil. It had gleaming limbs . . .*

At the other end of the room a ramp leads up to a large opening in which great gleaming cranks revolve, rising and falling; two great steam chests vent white plumes of steam alternately on either side, while beyond them more workers stand at panels, jerking like puppets as they throw switches and move levers.

We see one of the steam chests with the ramp in the foreground, the puppet-like workers beyond.

Three workers stand at their panels; white plumes rise from the steam chests in the foreground, while the great cranks revolve on the right.

The great nuts securing the front of the one the steam chests appear just in front of camera.

Six workers stand at their panels, three above another three.

Resume on the screen: the steam pours from the steam chests, the workers jerk at their panels and the great cranks revolve in the centre of the shot.

In one part of the machine room, a worker stands with his back to us in front of a vast panel covered in dials, levers, switches and flashing lights. In the centre of the panel is a kind of giant thermometer with jagged arrows indicating the danger level at the top. The worker rushes from one side to the other, throwing levers and switches in a frenzied rhythm.

> *He was wearing the uniform of all the workmen of Metropolis: from throat to ankle, the dark blue linen, bare feet in the hard shoes, hair tightly pressed down by the black cap . . .*

In the last stages of exhaustion he struggles to reach a switch . . .

While the thermometer begins to rise slowly towards the danger point.

As the worker struggles to reach his switch, a light glows on the panel in front of him.

He hangs from the machinery, looking up in horror at the thermometer off-screen . . .

While the temperature on the thermometer continues to rise relentlessly.

The worker jerks in frenzied despair and reaches up towards the panel.

His hand falls slackly on a valve . . .

The temperature rises . . .

While on the Pater Noster machine the steam puffs from the steam chests, the great cranks revolve and the twelve men jerk at their panels on either side.

The thermometer has now almost risen to the danger point . . .

And on the Pater Noster machine, everything is working in a frenzied rhythm.

Freder is still standing beside the concrete plinth, gazing up in awe at the scene in front of him.

The workers' movements become more and more frenzied as the cranks still turn and the plumes of steam arise in the foreground.

The thermometer reaches the critical level . . .

And a cloud of steam suddenly bursts forth from the maw of the Pater Noster machine.

One of the workers at his panel is thrown backwards by another blast.

Freder runs forward with a shout of alarm, one hand raised.

The great machine is seen from below; the workers leap from their posts as the whole room fills with steam.

Steam whirls round one of the great chests in the foreground; the figure of a worker drops from somewhere up above.

The dark figures of workers begin to drop like ripe fruit from their positions on the control panel high above the floor, as the steam continues to spurt and swirl around the great machine.

A worker stands trying to free himself from his smouldering overalls as several more run past in the foreground.

Freder is seen sitting back on the floor, obviously blown over by the blast. He suddenly starts to his knees.

The Pater Noster machine is seen from below. Most of the lights in the room have gone out and clouds of steam swirl across a white luminous expanse in the centre of the shot. Suddenly, in the centre, a vast grotesque face appears from out of the steam; the aperture with the revolving cranks becomes a gaping mouth with a row of teeth at the bottom and a flight of steps leading up to it.

Freder leans forward, staring in horror at this vision as he shouts:

TITLE: 'MOLOCH!'

Resume on the scene. The steam-filled room gradually fades away around the gaping face and two priests appear standing in the gateway of its mouth, their arms raised in attitudes of pagan worship. Freder crouches against the wall, staring in horror. He raises his arms as if trying to ward off the vision.

Again we see the gaping maw of the beast; the priests stand on either side with their arms raised, while gladiatorial figures hurl struggling, half-naked workers in amongst the gleaming cranks, which continue to rise and fall amid clouds of smoke and steam.

Resume on Freder, starting back in horror.

Long shot of the machine room; in the foreground the great steam chests puff out plumes of steam, while in the centre the guards shove a column of half-naked workers up the steps; a long column of workers in their dark uniforms march up in formation behind them and disappear row by row beneath the revolving cranks.

Freder is still kneeling on the ground in horror; with staring eyes he reaches out a hand . . .

Suddenly, the vision has faded, and we see the machine room in reality. The clouds of steam have dispersed and the cranks are stationary. Workers hurry to and fro helping their injured mates or carrying them on stretchers, while twelve new workers take up their positions on the sides of the great machine.

Freder cowers back against the wall of the machine room as a procession of the dead and wounded files slowly past in the foreground. He starts forward across the flagged floor to look at a figure on a stretcher.

We return to the machine as the last injured worker is helped away. The new shift are at their positions; the great cranks begin to turn again and plumes of steam emerge alternately from the great chests on either side.

Freder watches the spectacle for a moment, then he suddenly turns and runs off.

We look down some steps towards a large white chauffeur-driven car in the street. Trolleys laden with crates pass in the background as Freder rushes down the steps towards the car.

Seen through the car window Freder rushes up, flings open the door and addresses the driver.

Title : 'To my father !'

He gets in and slams the door and the car drives off.

In the great city, the car speeds across a bridge thrown between towering factory and office blocks, while slow-moving trucks carry workers along an elevated road beneath.

The canyon-like walls of the city blocks rise far above any street level. Cars and trains speed along overhead tracks, aeroplanes circle like moths . . .

While far below, the ground is alive with ant-like movement and activity.

Again we look through the canyon-like streets; far above all else, storey upon storey, rises the building known as the 'New Tower of Babel'.

> *In the brain-pan of this New Tower of Babel lived the man who was himself the Brain of Metropolis . . .*

The scene changes to a vast office. A great window looks out over the city in the background, while in the foreground is a vast semi-circular desk with clocks and writing materials on it and a couple of thickly upholstered armchairs at a table beyond. A thin, gaunt-looking man, wearing a Twenties-style sports jacket, walks across the room, wagging a finger as he dictates to his secretaries off-screen.

> *The brain-pan of the New Tower of Babel was peopled with numbers . . . From an invisible source the numbers dropped rhythmically down through the cooled air of the room, being collected, as in a water-basin, at the table at which the great brain of Metropolis worked, becoming objective under the pencils of his secretaries.*

One of the secretaries, Joseph, is feverishly noting down a series of symbols and figures which appear on a moving indicator on the wall behind him. He finishes one note pad, throws it down, picks up another, continues to write feverishly before the symbols disappear from view.

Meanwhile the gaunt-looking man walks to and fro, dictating. He comes towards camera and pauses, hand raised, searching for a word.

TITLE : JOHN FREDERSEN, THE MASTER OF METROPOLIS.

The Master stands with one finger raised, then turns suddenly at a noise off-screen.

On the other side of the office is a pair of great swing doors. One of them is hurled open and Freder rushes into the room.

TITLE : 'FATHER!'

Fredersen now has his back to us. With a sideways glance, he gestures to his son, indicating that he should not be interrupted.

Freder stands in the doorway, arms outstretched towards his father off-screen. Suddenly he starts—and puts out a hand to stop the door from banging behind him.

> *Whenever he entered this room he was once more a boy of ten years old, his chief characteristic uncertainty before the great concentrated, almighty certainty, which was called John Fredersen, and was his father . . .*

Meanwhile Fredersen finds the word he is searching for . . . and begins to dictate again.

At a table near the big desk are three secretaries. They jerk to life in unison and take down what the Master is saying in large ledgers . . .

> *Although sitting as immovable as statues, of which only the writing fingers of the right hand stirred, yet each single one, with sweat-bedewed brow and parted lips, seemed the personification of Breathlessness.*

Fredersen walks away from us towards the window, still dictating . . . While Freder, his hand on the doorknob, stares at his father with an agonised expression.

At the side of the room, Joseph is watching him in alarm. Now he turns, puts down his notebook and shuts off the indicator on the wall.

Freder is frozen in horror at the memory of what he has seen. And when Joseph comes up and anxiously enquires what is the matter, he clutches the secretary by the arm and pours out his tale.

Fredersen, on the other side of the room, pauses in his dictation and glances towards his son . . .

While Freder, with his arm round Joseph's shoulder, describes the accident with extravagant gestures.

Fredersen watches his son for a moment with a stern expression, walks off as he continues to dictate, then reappears, pauses and looks off at the two men.

Freder is still describing the accident to Joseph with sweeping gestures, an expression of horror on his face.

Seen in medium close-up, Fredersen speaks:

TITLE : 'SUCH ACCIDENTS ARE UNAVOIDABLE.'

We see the other two men. Freder whips round; his face lights up at the sound of his father's voice. He rushes towards him, shouting: *'Father!'*

It was as though the son, up-rooting and tearing loose his whole ego, threw himself, with a gesture of utter self-exposure, upon his father.

He runs up to Fredersen and grabs him by the shoulders, speaking urgently; he clasps his hands to his head in horror. His father looks sternly off at Joseph, puts out a restraining hand to his son, then walks off.

Joseph is standing to one side of the swing doors. He backs away nervously as Fredersen comes towards him.

Hands in pockets, Fredersen sternly faces Joseph, who is seen in back view in the foreground. The Master of Metropolis speaks:

TITLE: 'WHY WAS MY SON ALLOWED TO GO INTO THE MACHINE ROOMS?'

Seen in reverse shot, Joseph stares at Fredersen, lost for words. Fredersen faces camera. Joseph shakes his head as he replies. Joseph hurries out of the door. Fredersen turns, hands in pockets, and comes back into the centre of the room.

Freder rushes up to his father and we see the two of them from the side. Fredersen tries to placate his son who speaks to him urgently, clutching his arms. Fredersen asks:

TITLE: 'WHY DID YOU GO DOWN THERE?'

We resume on the two men as Freder replies:

TITLE: 'I WANTED TO SEE WHAT MY BROTHERS LOOKED LIKE.'

As Freder continues to speak, his father puts out a restraining hand, then gestures to the secretaries off-screen.

Seen from above, the secretaries throw down their pencils in unison, and get ready to leave.

Camera pans slightly as Fredersen pushes his son towards an armchair, putting a soothing hand on his shoulder. Freder claps his hands to his head and sinks into the armchair as he speaks in horrified tones.

'I went through the machine-rooms—they were like temples. All the great gods were living in white temples. I saw Baal and Moloch, Huilzilopochtli and Durgha . . .'

His father listens, gazing off-screen.

'I saw Juggernaut's divine car and the Towers of Silence,

38

Mahomet's curved sword, and the crosses of Golgotha. And all machines, machines, machines . . .'

Freder, in the armchair, clasps his arms to his chest as he continues to recite his vision with staring eyes.

'And near the god-machines, the slaves of the god-machines: the men who were as though crushed between machine companionability and machine solitude . . .'

And still his father listens.

'. . . They have no loads to carry: the machine carries the loads. They have not to lift and push: the machine lifts and pushes. They have nothing else to do but eternally one and the same thing, each in his place, each at his machine.'

Fredersen is standing over his son, who sits with head bowed in the armchair at bottom of frame. He turns and takes a few steps towards the window. Freder stops in his narration and starts up after him, crying out: *'Father!'*

The Master of Metropolis stands by the wall, hands behind his back, unmoving and unmoved. Freder comes up and clasps him round the shoulder, pointing urgently through the window off-screen.

TITLE: 'IT WAS THEIR HANDS THAT BUILT THIS CITY OF YOURS, FATHER.'

TITLE: 'BUT WHERE DO THE HANDS BELONG IN YOUR SCHEME?'

We look out over the vast city from the great window of the office. A montage shot shows tall buildings, rising like mountains in every direction.

Dissolve to a similar montage shot—more monolithic blocks on multiple levels, light shining from their windows.

Then we look down on the top of the great Tower of Babel where Fredersen's office is.

TITLE: 'IN THEIR PROPER PLACE—THE DEPTHS.'

We see a lift cage descending with the outgoing shift of workers, standing in serried ranks, their heads bowed. The picture goes dim as the lift descends into darkness. Fade out.

In the office, Freder is still staring intently ahead of him. He speaks to his father, who is standing just behind him with head bowed, his back turned to his son.

39

TITLE: 'WHAT WILL YOU DO IF THEY TURN AGANST YOU SOME DAY?'

One hand on his hip, Fredersen stands looking out of the window, while on the right, Freder gazes into emptiness, pursuing his apocalyptic vision of the future. His father turns towards him and shakes his head with a reassuring smile.

Seen from above, a light flashes on and off insistently on one of the control panels.

While Freder stands with his arms outstretched, his father walks off towards his desk.

He stands at the vast, curved desk and presses a button on the control panel.

We look out from behind the desk to the window overlooking the city. Night is falling. As his father presses the button in the foreground, Freder steps up to the window and looks out as long black curtains begin to sweep across it, cutting off the view. Fredersen turns and looks off-screen . . .

As Joseph hurries in through the big swing doors of the office and announces:

TITLE: 'THE FOREMAN FROM THE CENTRAL DYNAMO ROOM IS HERE WITH AN URGENT MESSAGE.'

Fredersen tells Joseph to let him in; then he sits down at his desk as the secretary opens the door in the background and Grot, the foreman, hurries into the room. He pauses awkwardly—a thick-set figure with a black beard, wearing the overalls of a worker. Then Fredersen beckons him forward and he comes round the desk toward us.

Fredersen sits at his desk, his eyes boring into the foreman off-screen. With a nod of his head, he tells him to speak.

Grot pauses, looking at the Master of Metropolis; then he suddenly leans forwards, holding out a crumpled piece of paper.

TITLE: 'MORE OF THOSE PLANS, SIR.'

Fredersen's expression hardens. He looks sideways and taps a hand reflectively on the arm of his chair.

Joseph, who is standing by the door, hurries forward, then pauses, swallowing hard.

Fredersen, at his desk, looks sternly off at Joseph, while Grot leans across in the foreground and places the piece of paper on the desk. He withdraws again while Fredersen gets up and leans forward, looking down at the paper.

We look down at two identical plans, heavily folded, covered with arrows and figures.

They were no larger than a man's hand, bearing neither print nor script, being covered over and over with the tracing of a strange symbol and an apparently half-destroyed plan. Ways seemed to be indicated, seeming to be false ways, but they all led one way; to a place that was filled with crosses . . .

Fredersen looks up again sternly.

Grot tosses his head as he speaks gruffly.

TITLE: 'THEY WERE FOUND ON TWO OF THE MEN WHO WERE KILLED TODAY.'

Fredersen gazes intently at Grot, in back view in the foreground, then fixes his steely eyes on Joseph off-screen. He speaks . . .

And Joseph hurries forward nervously.

Freder is beside one of the armchairs, listening. He too starts forward.

Standing at his desk, Fredersen gazes off at his son, while he holds out the plans to Joseph behind him and says:

TITLE: 'JOSEPH, WHY WAS IT NOT YOU WHO BROUGHT ME THESE PLANS?'

Without looking at him, Fredersen holds up the plans towards his secretary. Joseph fingers the edge of the desk nervously. He has nothing to say.

A closer shot of Fredersen, holding up the plans, as he continues to gaze sternly off towards his son.

Joseph opens his mouth nervously, but no words come out.

Fredersen is looking sterner every moment. He folds up the plans and addresses Joseph off-screen.

TITLE: 'YOU ARE DISMISSED. GO TO THE G BANK FOR THE BALANCE OF YOUR WAGES.'

The young man stood motionless. Three, four, five, six seconds ticked away. Two empty eyes burnt in the chalky face of the

41

young man, impressing their brand of fear upon Freder's vision.

Joseph bows slowly to Fredersen's back.

And Freder, standing just in front of the armchair, drops his head, overcome.

While Grot looks on in the background, Joseph turns and walks slowly and painfully away from the two men.

At the door, he staggers like a man who has been hit, reaches blindly for the doorknob, then walks stiffly out of the room. The door swings to behind him.

Fredersen stands in back view at his desk, his son opposite him, head bowed. Suddenly Freder looks up and addresses his father, pointing urgently towards the door.

TITLE: 'FATHER, DON'T YOU REALIZE WHAT IT MEANS TO BE DISMISSED BY YOU?'

He leans anxiously across the desk. Fredersen shrugs, and his son backs away from him, a look of hopelessness in his eyes. Then he suddenly turns . . .

And dashes off past Grot.

The Master of Metropolis turns to follow his son with his eyes . . .

As Freder rushes out of the door.

Joseph is staggering down the stairs from the Master's office. He sways to and fro as if drunk or in a daze, then after a moment's reflection reaches slowly into his pocket.

At that moment, Freder comes pelting down the stairs after him. Joseph slowly pulls a gun out of his pocket.

Freder runs down the stairs towards camera with his arms outstreched . . .

And just as Joseph is about to put the gun to his temple, rushes up behind him and grabs it away.

We see the two men as Freder forces Joseph's arm down and speaks to him urgently, looking him in the eye.

Back in the great office, the Master of Metropolis gazes sternly towards the door through which his son has made his hurried exit. In the background Grot shifts uncomfortably.

A shot of the door.

Fredersen continues to gaze at it for a moment, then turns away. On the stairs, Joseph is standing with his arms pressed against the

42

wall in an attitude of desperation; he slowly turns towards Freder as the latter addresses him.

TITLE: 'JOSEPH, I NEED YOUR HELP.'

Freder holds out his hands to Joseph in a gesture of friendship. Joseph looks down and suddenly clasps them in his.
Facing camera, Freder explains to Joseph what he must do.

TITLE: 'I HAVE FAR TO GO TODAY—ALONE, INTO THE DEPTHS—TO MY BROTHERS.'

An iron staircase leads down to a landing in the bowels of the city. Freder comes down the staircase and stands looking around him at the bottom. He pauses, notices a door in the background and goes up to it . . .

> *He had hesitated before opening that door. For a weird existence went on behind that door. There was howling. There was panting. There was whistling. The whole building groaned. An incessant trembling ran through the walls and floor. And amidst it all there was not one human sound. Only the things and the empty air roared. Men in the room on the other side of this door had powerless sealed lips. But for these men's sakes Freder had come.*

. . . Finally, he pushes open the door, and great clouds of steam billow out at him. With a determined air he strides in through the doorway.

> *Boiling air smote him, groping at his eyes that he saw nothing. Gradually he regained his sight.*

Reverse shot from inside. First the screen is filled with swirling steam, then it clears slightly as Freder comes toward us, staring at the spectacle which meets his eyes.

> *The room was dimly lighted and the ceiling, which looked as though it could carry the weight of the entire earth, seemed perpetually to be falling down.*

We are in a great steam-filled cavern, with workers trudging about their tasks in the gloom. A worker passes by on a self-propelled truck.

Freder puts a hand to his head and gazes in awe at the scene.

> *Heat spat from the walls in which the furnaces were roaring. The odour of oil, which whistled with heat, hung in thick*

43

layers in the room . . .

The workers trudge to and fro through the steam-filled room, with heads bent, and jerky, mechanical steps . . .

Their movements, the soundlessness of their inaudible slipping past, had something of the black ghostliness of deep-sea divers.

. . . In the background we see a man feverishly moving the hands on a vast dial, in a sequence prescribed by lights flashing around the edge.

He was wearing the uniform of all the workmen of Metropolis: from throat to ankle, the dark blue linen, bare feet in the hard shoes, hair tightly pressed down by the black cap.

Freder gazes across at the man and starts forward.

Thin clouds of steam swirl across in front of the man as he feverishly turns the pointers on the great dial. Freder approaches hesitantly from the foreground.

Still the man clutches unceasingly at the lever . . .

While Freder steps forward and leans against a pillar, staring in horror and amazement.

The man at the dial pauses for a fraction of a second and feverishly wipes his forehead and face. He is obviously on the verge of collapse.

Freder leans forward anxiously.

The man at the machine turns to look at Freder, then suddenly staggers backwards in a faint. Freder rushes up and catches him in his arms, while the relinquished pointers swing loosely on the dial. As he looks round for help, the man regains consciousness and frenziedly tries to return to his post, shouting:

TITLE : 'THE MACHINE ! SOMEONE MUST STAY WITH THE MACHINE.'

Freder tries to restrain the worker as he struggles furiously, pointing towards the dial behind them. Freder speaks:

TITLE : 'I WILL STAY AT THE MACHINE.'

As he finishes, a light flashes insistently on the dial behind him.

With one hand, Freder leans the worker gently up against a pillar, then he turns and frenziedly starts to move the pointers round the dial as the lights flash on and off in a rapid sequence. At the same time he turns and addresses the worker.

'We shall now exchange lives . . . You take mine, I yours. I shall take your place at the machine. You go quietly out in my clothes. Nobody noticed me when I came here. Nobody will notice you when you go.'

A closer shot of the two of them. Freder continues to move the pointers round the dial as he speaks to the worker in friendly tones. The worker listens attentively while the steam swirls across in front of them.

TITLE: IN THE MIDDLE OF THE CITY WAS AN OLD HOUSE.

It was older than the town . . . It had lived through the time of smoke and soot. Every year which passed over the city seemed to creep, when dying, into this house, so that at last it was a cemetery—a coffin, filled with dead tens of years . . .

A low angle shot shows the house with its steeply pitched roof, surrounded by the towering blocks of the city with light streaming from their windows. It stands dark and unlit, the front wall blank except for a wooden door.

Set into the black wood of the door stood, copper-red, myster-

ious, the seal of Solomon, the pentagram.

TITLE : HERE LIVED ROTWANG, THE INVENTOR.

We now see Rotwang himself, wearing a dark smock, poring over a diagram on his work table. He is old and grey-haired, with beetling brows, and his right hand is artificial, made of a dark, glistening material. Rotwang looks up and mutters . . .

As a small hunchbacked servant appears at the top of a spiral metal staircase and announces :

TITLE : 'JOHN FREDERSEN !'

We return to Freder at the dial in the machine rooms. He looks exhausted, and is now wearing the dark overalls of the worker as he speaks urgently to the latter off-screen.

> *When you reach the street take a car. You will find more than enough money in my pockets . . . Drive to the Ninetieth Block . . . then find your way to the seventh floor of the seventh house. A man called Joseph lives there. You are to go to him. Tell him I sent you . . .'*

We see the worker, now wearing Freder's white silk clothing. He

46

nods several times, looking at the address on a piece of paper in his hand, then, suddenly noticing the worker's cap which he is still holding, he hands it to Freder off-screen.

Freder, at the dial face, takes the cap as the worker hands it to him. He looks at it—on it is written the name GEORG and the number 1811. Freder smiles, then puts on the cap.

We see the two men at the dial face. Freder continues to work the pointers feverishly, while Georg looks at the paper in his hand. Steam swirls around them as they exchange a last few words. Georg pauses, overcome by his new freedom, then rushes off in the foreground.

In Rotwang's house, the inventor and the Master of Metropolis stand facing one another. Rotwang is talking agitatedly, gesticulating with his artificial hand. Fredersen takes hold of the hand and looks at it, while Rotwang gazes at him with a wild gleam in his eye.

TITLE: 'AT LAST MY WORK IS READY.'

Rotwang leans forward, waving his artificial finger right in front of camera, his eyes wild and staring.

TITLE: 'I HAVE CREATED A MACHINE IN THE IMAGE OF MAN, THAT NEVER TIRES OR MAKES A MISTAKE.'

As Rotwang continues to gesture fanatically towards the ceiling, Fredersen turns his steely gaze on the inventor and demands to know what he is talking about. Rotwang's face takes on a sly expression as he says:

TITLE: 'NOW WE HAVE NO FURTHER USE FOR LIVING WORKERS.'

Fredersen looks at him from under his bushy eyebrows, and bites his lip.

Resume on the two of them. Rotwang points off-screen, then goes out of shot.

He reappears at the top of a spiral staircase which leads up into his workshop. It is a large room filled with strange apparatuses, retorts on stands, coiled cables and glowing tubes. In one corner is a tall glass cylinder, filled with a bubbling liquid. Rotwang goes off and Fredersen comes up after him, looks round the room and follows him out of shot.

The two of them are seen from behind as they walk towards a curtain at one side of the studio. The inventor flings aside the curtain and looks triumphantly at Fredersen. In the background is a gleaming robot, seated on a plinth, with a narrow platform running out from the front of it. Rotwang turns a switch and a light glows from under the plinth. Then he gestures Fredersen towards him.

Fredersen steps forward, and stares at the being which sits before him.

A closer shot of the gleaming robot, seated on its plinth.

> *The being was, indubitably, a woman . . .But, although it was a woman, it was not human. The body seemed as though made of crystal . . . Cold streamed from the glazen skin which did not contain a drop of blood.*

We now see Fredersen and Rotwang, backs to camera, with the robot in the background. Fredersen makes as if to speak, but Rotwang restrains him with a gesture and, turning to the robot, raises one hand in the air. Suddenly the gleaming figure starts to move. Slowly and smoothly, it places its hand on the arm of its

seat and rises to its feet. The Master of Metropolis starts forwards, then begins to back away as the figure walks slowly along the platform towards him, swinging its articulated hips.

Rotwang stands in the foreground as the robot towers over him and slowly turns her head. She is made of gleaming metal, with sculptured breasts and ribs and heavy articulated joints at the elbows . . .

> *But the being had no face . . . The skull was bald, nose, lips, temples merely traced. Eyes, as though painted on closed lids, stared unseeingly, with an expression of calm madness, at the man . . .*

. . . Rotwang speaks to her, gesturing towards Fredersen off-screen. The robot turns her head to the front and walks forward again.

We now see Fredersen again as the robot reaches the end of the platform, turns towards him and slowly raises one hand.

Seen from below, the robot towers over Fredersen, and offers him a metallic handshake.

Reverse shot as Fredersen backs away, almost in alarm.

We see the two of them again as Rotwang appears from the right, a maniac gleam in his eye, and gestures aloft with his artificial hand.

TITLE: 'ISN'T IT WORTH THE LOSS OF A HAND TO HAVE CREATED THE WORKERS OF THE FUTURE—THE MACHINE MEN!'

The robot towers above Rotwang as he looks from Fredersen to her and back again, then gestures with both arms as he speaks.

TITLE: 'GIVE ME ANOTHER 24 HOURS, AND I'LL GIVE YOU A MACHINE WHICH NO ONE WILL BE ABLE TO TELL FROM A HUMAN BEING.'

Rotwang stands with his arms triumphantly outstretched, while behind him towers the robot, her hand still extended towards Fredersen on the left. The inventor gestures extravagantly as he continues to talk wildly of his invention . . .

> *'You can test it, John Fredersen: it is faultless. A little cool— I admit, that comes of the material, which is my secret. But she is not yet completely finished. She is not yet discharged from the workshop of her creator . . . I do not want to set her free from me. That is why I have not given her a face. You*

must give her that, John Fredersen. For you were the one to order the new being.'

. . . He jabs a finger at Fredersen's chest. The Master of Metropolis looks thoughtful.

And the robot's unseeing eyes stare blankly from the sculptured metal head.

In the steam-filled machine room, Freder continues to move the pointers round the dial, his actions visibly slower as exhaustion overcomes him.

We return to Fredersen and Rotwang. The curtains have now been drawn again, hiding the robot. Fredersen strides up to the inventor. Rotwang looks sideways at Fredersen as the latter addressed him.

TITLE : 'AS ALWAYS, WHEN MY EXPERTS FAIL I COME TO YOU FOR ADVICE.'

Rotwang looks away with a smirk as Fredersen pulls the two diagrams presented to him by Grot out of his pocket. He unfolds them and holds them out to the inventor as he says :

TITLE : 'FOR MONTHS NOW, WE HAVE BEEN FINDING THESE PLANS IN THE WORKERS' CLOTHING. WHAT DO THEY MEAN?'

At the dial, Freder pulls a handkerchief from the pocket of the workers' overalls, to wipe the sweat from his neck and face. A piece of paper falls out of the pocket, and as he is putting the handkerchief away again, Freder notices it on the ground.

Freder's hand picks up the piece of paper, which has landed by his foot. He bends down to look at it—it is another of the plans.

At that moment, a maintenance worker carrying a spanner and a couple of oil cans descends a steel ladder into the machine room. He looks off at Freder . . .

While Freder continues to move the pointers feverishly in response to the flashing lights, simultaneously glancing at the paper clasped in his hand.

The maintenance worker reaches the bottom of the ladder . . .

As Freder, still looking at the plan, shakes his head.

A closer shot as he turns back to the dial, still looking at the plan. The maintenance worker now steps from the ladder and walks slowly off to the right.

Freder is seen from behind, still looking at the piece of paper. The maintenance worker appears on the left, looking back furtively over his shoulder.

Freder turns as he addresses him in an undertone.

TITLE: 'AT TWO—AT THE END OF THIS SHIFT—SHE HAS CALLED ANOTHER MEETING.'

With another furtive glance around him, the maintenance worker disappears. Freder is bewildered. He looks at the piece of paper in his hand again, and calls after the worker: *'What?'*

Then he turns back to the dial and frenziedly starts moving the pointers again.

We move back to Rotwang's study. Fredersen is sitting in a wing chair in the foreground, while beyond him Rotwang stands behind his work table, going over one of the diagrams with a pair of dividers. There are shelves of leather-bound books in the background, while a curious illuminated spiral stands on one end of the work table. Rotwang consults a weighty volume at his side.

Seen in a closer shot, Fredersen sits waiting; he glances at the inventor off-screen, then down at his watch.

The watch says just past ten o'clock.

We return to Freder in the machine room . . .

> *The man before the machine was no longer a human being. Merely a dripping piece of exhaustion, from the pores of which the last powers of volition were oozing out in large drops of sweat.*

. . . He leans back towards camera, clinging limply to the pointers of the dial, and clasps an arm to his forehead.

We see the ten hour clock on the wall of Fredersen's office. There is half an hour to go to the end of the shift.

Freder, in the steam-filled machine room, is so exhausted that he can hardly move the pointers. Every movement is a gigantic effort . . .

And meanwhile, a giant thermometer on the wall rises slowly to the danger point.

Freder staggers to and fro, then suddenly sinks to his knees with one of the pointers held above his head. The glowing figures of the ten hour clock fade into superimposition on the dial face and one of the pointers starts to tick round as if it were the second hand.

Freder glances up and grabs hold of the moving hand.

We see his face twisted in agony, the glowing figures behind.
Now he is on his knees in front of the dial, his face contorted as he
grasps at the moving pointer.
He looks up at the pointer with staring eyes . . .
His mouth opens and he shouts out in agony . . .
Both his arms are outstretched, holding the pointers as if he were
suspended from them, crucified; again he shouts in agony:

TITLE: 'FATHER, FATHER—I DID NOT KNOW THAT TEN HOURS CAN
BE TORTURE.'

The pointer slips down in his hand as he continues to shout . . .
While we cut to a shot of the great steam sirens outside in the city.
It is dark, and the towering blocks of Metropolis loom on either
side, lights gleaming from their myriad windows. Suddenly the
sirens blast loudly, spouting out jets of steam.
Freder is now practically lying on the floor in front of the dial. He
staggers to his feet and leans against the wall, gasping, as the siren
sounds his deliverance. Another worker steps into view from the
left, takes his place at the dial and starts feverishly moving the

pointers. Three workers from the outgoing shift move past in the foreground, their heads bowed, completely spent. Freder trudges after them . . .

While the steam sirens continue to sound in the night.

We return to Rotwang's study. Fredersen looks up from his chair in the foreground as Rotwang inspects the plan he has given him, and says:

Title: 'These are the plans of the ancient catacombs—far below the lowest levels of the workers' city.'

Rotwang closes the book he has been referring to and goes to put it on the shelf behind him, while Fredersen picks up the piece of paper and looks at it thoughtfully.

We see the plan in Fredersen's hand.

Then we cut to a line of workers filing down a dimly-lit flight of steps past a rocky wall. With an even, weary tread, they descend into the catacombs. The plan remains superimposed across the corners of the picture.

Dissolve back to the plan again.

Fredersen sits facing us in his chair, gazing down at the plan in his hands. He lets it drop and stares ahead of him as he says:

TITLE: 'WHAT IS IT DOWN THERE THAT INTERESTS THE WORKERS?'

Rotwang glances off at Fredersen, puts a book back on the shelf, then turns to face him, leaning back against the bookcase.

Fredersen leaps to his feet in the foreground as the inventor comes slowly forward to face him on the other side of the desk. Without a word Rotwang takes a couple of electric torches from a drawer, hands one across to Fredersen, then gestures towards one corner of the room. Fredersen turns and looks off . . .

To where a staircase leads downwards out of the study. Preceded by his shadow, Rotwang appears from the left and goes down the stairs, turning to beckon Fredersen on. The latter appears in back view and follows him down.

The two men arrive at the bottom of the spiral staircase. Rotwang takes a key from a hook on the wall and goes through a door.

We are now in a large cellar beneath Rotwang's house, with several doors leading off it. As Fredersen comes through the doorway in the background, Rotwang opens a large trap-door in the centre of the floor and shines his torch into it. Fredersen goes down a few steps into the hole, shining his torch downwards to inspect what lies below. Then, after exchanging a few words with Rotwang, he goes on down out of sight. The inventor follows and closes the trap-door behind them.

Beneath the cellar, a well worn staircase leads down into the gloom of the catacombs. The two men descend the steps toward us, shining their torches in front of them.

Meanwhile, somewhere below the city, a file of workers are trudging down another gloomy staircase, lit by candles.

Rotwang and Fredersen continue on their way, shining their torches in front of them. The passage is arched above their heads and there are large blocks of masonry on either side.

The workers trudge onwards, dragging their feet with exhaustion. One of them staggers and is helped along by his fellows; it is Freder.

> *He walked and walked in smouldering weariness. The way would never, never come to an end. He did not know where he was walking. He heard the tramp of those who were walk-*

54

ing with him like the sound of perpetually falling water.
The camera tracks slowly out in front of the workers as they come
down the steps into a large, dimly lit cavern . . .

> *A vault, like the vault of a sepulchre, human heads so closely*
> *crowded together as to produce the effect of clods on a freshly*
> *ploughed field. All heads turned towards one point.*

. . . The staggering figure of Freder approaches in the centre of
the shot. He clutches a hand to his chest; his head is bowed; he is
looking at the ground.
Still clutching at his chest, Freder slowly looks up . . . and suddenly
stares at what he sees off-screen.

> *Candles burnt with sword-like flames. Slender, lustrous swords*
> *of light stood in a circle round the head of a girl, whose voice*
> *was as the amen of God . . .*

We look across the cavern, over the heads of the workers. In the
background a flight of steps leads up to an altar laden with brightly
burning candles. Large crosses stand behind and on either side,
and in the very centre of the shot, just in front of the altar, is the
girl whom we first saw in the Eternal Gardens. Slowly, she spreads

her arms wide in a gesture of welcome.

Freder can only stare in awe and wonderment. Slowly, he raises a hand and takes off his worker's cap.

Maria stares straight at camera, goodness and tenderness shining from her Madonna-like eyes; then she spreads her arms wide, looking up to heaven, and begins to speak.

Freder is seen from above. All the workers around him are standing or kneeling, their heads bent. He alone gazes up in wonderment at the vision off-screen, then slowly sinks to his knees, spreading his arms wide in a gesture of supplication.

> *He longed to stroke with his hands the stones on which he knelt. God—God—God beat the heart in his breast, and every throb was a thank-offering. He looked at the girl, and yet he did not see her. He saw only a shimmer; he knelt before it.*

Meanwhile, in a smaller cavern above the gathering, light from the altar candles streams in through a lozenge-shaped hole. Rotwang, who has put his torch down on a stone, goes over to the aperture in the background and beckons to Fredersen. The Master of Metropolis appears, puts down his torch beside Rotwang's and goes to join him. They stand with their backs to us, looking through the hole.

Far beneath them, Maria stands at the altar, flanked by blocks of masonry, her arms spread wide as she addresses the workers gathered below.

The cavern is now filled with workers, sitting, standing, perched on blocks of stone. They are all staring straight at camera, in the direction of Maria.

Brilliantly lit by the candles behind her, Maria gazes up to heaven. She looks down at the workers again, then raises one hand and speaks.

Title : 'Today I will tell you the story of the Tower of Babel.'

(The following scenes, telling the story of the Tower of Babel, are all characterized by an irridescent iris effect round the edge of the picture.)

A tall, grey-haired figure in glittering robes stands with folded arms on a dais, gazing upwards. Behind him are the star-studded heavens, in front of him his friends. At first kneeling with heads bowed, they look up as he addresses them.

Title : 'Let us build a tower whose summit will touch the skies—'

The figure spreads his arms as he continues.

Title : '—and on it we will inscribe : "Great is the world and its Creator, and great is Man".'

Against the same star-lit background, the vast Tower of Babel rises to the heavens, its spiral terraces dwarfing the countryside beneath it. Then the background dissolves away to show the tower's creators seated on a stone bench around what now appears as a model of the tower. They are all in attitudes of profound thought. The grey-haired man, who is seated on the left, leans forward and shakes his head.

Title : 'Those who conceived the idea of this tower could not have built it themselves, so they hired thousands of others to build it for them.'

A montage shot shows five ant-like columns of half naked workers advancing and dissolving into one another in the centre of the screen. Their shaved heads are bent towards camera as they shuffle forwards.

Title : 'But these toilers knew nothing of the dream of those who planned the tower.'

We now see the Tower of Babel, surrounded by a vast, brilliant halo of light. Beneath it, the grey-haired figure kneels in an attitude of worship.

Title : 'While those who conceived the tower did not concern themselves with the workers who built it.'

Seen from above, thousands of half-naked workers toil over rough stony ground, hauling on ropes. They are dragging a vast block of stone which towers right out of the picture.
We see the workers at the foot of the monolith as they drag it painfully along. They raise their shaven heads towards camera and shout and scream in agony.

Title : 'The hymns of praise of the few became the curses of the many.'

A vast flight of steps rises away from camera; at the top stands the thin, grey-haired figure of the tower's creator, brilliantly lit from behind. With sweeping gestures, he addresses a group of half-naked workers at the bottom of the steps in the foreground. As he continues to speak, the workers start to shout and wave their fists at him.

Title : 'BABEL.'

The workers continue to shake their fists, then suddenly surge forward up the steps. More and more workers swarm like ants from the bottom of the picture and soon the whole staircase is a sea of half-naked figures as they rush up and angrily surround the grey-haired figure at the top.
Now we see the tower itself surrounded by a halo of light. A forest of grasping hands reach up to it in silhouette, almost filling the screen.
Fade in to a shot against the starry heavens. In the centre stands

all that remains of the Tower of Babel—a vast pile of crumbling masonry—while across the sky above it stands the legend: 'GREAT IS THE WORLD AND ITS CREATOR, AND GREAT IS MAN.' The words fade out, leaving only the pile of ruined masonry against the starlit sky, then the entire picture fades out slowly.

Fade in again to Maria, the candles on the altar burning behind her. She stares straight ahead of her, speaking as if in a trance.

TITLE: 'BETWEEN THE BRAIN THAT PLANS AND THE HANDS THAT BUILD, THERE MUST BE A MEDIATOR.'

Maria stares straight at camera; she clasps both hands to her breast as she speaks earnestly and fervently.

TITLE: 'IT IS THE HEART THAT MUST BRING ABOUT AN UNDER-STANDING BETWEEN THEM.'

Resume on Maria as she finishes speaking.
> *She was silent. A breath like a sigh came up from the silent lips of the listeners.*

We see one of the workers, staring off at Maria. Then he clasps his hands together, bends his head and closes his eyes as if in prayer.

Two more workers do the same.

Camera tilts down with another worker as he sinks slowly to his knees and bows his head together with his colleagues.

The workers are seen from above, kneeling or sitting with their heads bent. One of them stands up slowly, resting his fists on the shoulders of the men who crouch before him, and asks:

TITLE: 'WHERE IS OUR MEDIATOR, MARIA?'

Maria is gazing straight at camera, still as if in a trance. She suddenly looks off to the left as the man addresses her.

The workers round Freder all raise their heads together. Freder himself glances sideways at the questioner, then looks up again towards the altar. A beatific expression comes over his face; he clenches his fists on his chest and murmurs: *'Me! . . . Me!'*

Her hands clasped to her heart, Maria raises her eyes to heaven and says:

TITLE : 'BE PATIENT, HE WILL SURELY COME.'

Resume on Maria, eyes and hands uplifted in a gesture of supplication . . .
While Freder beats his hands on his chest and falls forward, repeating to himself : *'Me! . . . Me!'*
Resume on the questioner, his hands on his fellow workers' shoulders. They are all leaning forward now, and there is a fanatical gleam in their eyes. One of them grasps the questioner's arm and suddenly points off towards Maria as he shouts out :

TITLE : 'WE WILL WAIT, BUT NOT FOR LONG.'

Behind them, in a vault that was shaped like a pointed devil's ear . . .
Camera pans with Fredersen as he backs away from the aperture which gives onto the cavern, his face stern. He murmurs to himself and clenches his fists as he turns away.
Rotwang, in back view, stands looking down through the aperture ; candlelight streams through from the altar below. The inventor turns at the sound of Fredersen's voice.

Fredersen stands looking down at him. His face is set, and he plunges his hands into his pockets as he says:

Title: 'Rotwang, make your Robot in the likeness of that girl.'

Rotwang is once more looking down through the aperture. He turns and backs against it, looking off at Fredersen. A gleam comes into his eyes.
Fredersen takes one hand from his pocket and clenches his fist in the air. He continues:

Title: 'Hide the girl in your house, I will send the robot down to the workers, to sow discord among them and destroy their confidence in Maria.'

Rotwang looks sideways at Fredersen, who brings down his clench-ed fist and turns towards the inventor, holding out his hand. Slowly looking him straight in the eye, Rotwang extends his artificial hand and encloses Fredersen's in a metallic grasp.

Title: 'Leave me here, John Fredersen.'

Fredersen stares at Rotwang as he finishes speaking, then goes off in the foreground. The circle of light from his torch passes over Rotwang's face as the inventor gazes after him, a fanatical gleam in his eye.

We look down on the cavern as seen from Rotwang's hiding place. The workers are all standing or kneeling with heads bent. Then they get up and, slowly and wearily, start to leave.

Rotwang is seen from below, through the aperture. He turns to look down into the cavern again.

Down below, only Maria now remains, standing at the altar, with Freder, a solitary figure, kneeling with his hands clasped to his chest. Maria turns and starts to come down from the altar.

Freder looks up, and sees . . .

Maria—in side view—coming down the steps.

He stretches out an arm in an imploring gesture, and suddenly calls after her.

Maria, who has not seen him, whips round at the sound of his voice . . .

While Freder gazes up at her, one hand outstretched, the other to his breast.

> *The girl's face was as a crystal, filled with snow. She made a movement as if for flight. But her knees would not obey her. Reeds which stand in troubled water do not tremble more than her shoulders trembled.*

Maria clutches a hand to her heart, starts forward, hesitates, love shining in her eyes.

Resume on Freder as he speaks.

> 'You . . .' said the man . . . 'You are really the great mediatress . . . you are all that is most sacred on earth . . .'

She moves out of shot towards him . . .

And Freder turns his eyes to follow her; his face lights up.

Soon from below, Maria advances towards him, the altar in the background. Her face fills the picture; her luminous Madonna-eyes gaze straight at camera . . .

While Freder gazes up at her as if in a trance, and speaks.

> '. . . You are all goodness . . . You are all grace . . . To doubt you is to doubt God . . .'

We now see the two of them, Maria facing camera. She puts her hands to her breast and speaks to him tenderly.

Now Freder faces us as he speaks to Maria, love shining in his eyes. Seen in back view she lays her hands on his shoulders.

'. . . *Maria—Maria—you called me—here I am!*'

Now facing us again, she gazes down into Freder's eyes, then slowly leans forward and kisses him tenderly on the cheek.

Then, in reverse shot, she draws away from him. Freder's eyes are closed in ecstasy; now he opens them and gazes up at her.

Facing us once more, she runs her hands over his hair, speaking to him tenderly.

We now see the two of them with the steps leading up to the altar behind. Freder gets up and stands over Maria, takes her hands in his.

Maria, facing us, leans towards Freder and speaks to him earnestly.

TITLE: 'UNTIL TOMORROW—IN THE CATHEDRAL.'

We see the two of them in profile, their hands clasped together. She pushes him gently but firmly away, speaking to him all the time. He backs away, stroking her arm in a last lingering contact, then clasps her hand and kisses it, and disappears. She stands with her hand raised in a gesture of farewell, while camera pans to bring her back into the centre of the shot. Overcome with emotion, she clasps her hands to her chest and closes her eyes.

Just outside the cavern, Rotwang peers round a corner, his face gleaming in the candle-light, his artificial hand glistening.

Maria's eyes are still closed in ecstasy. After a moment she opens them, pulls herself together, looks round and smiles to herself, then starts to descend some steps towards the bottom of the shot.

She walked on, smiling and not knowing she did it. She felt like singing. With an expression of happiness, which was still incredulous and yet complete, she said the name of her beloved over to herself.

She comes down some steps and turns to take a candle from a holder on the wall.

Then she comes towards the camera, holding the candle aloft.

Seen from above, Rotwang peers after her; suddenly he grabs a lump of rock out of the wall with his artificial hand and lets it fall to the ground.

The piece of stone lands with a thump . . .

And Maria, walking away with the candle, whips round in alarm;

64

she looks back towards . . .

The archway where Rotwang was standing, dimly lit in the candlelight. There is no one there.

> *But suddenly there came a cold draught of air which made the hair at her neck quiver, and a hand of snow ran down her back . . .*

Maria swallows hard, then draws her shawl protectively around her, her eyes riveted to the spot.

Seen from above, she looks round anxiously, then turns and walks off to the left, holding her candle aloft.

Now she comes into view from the right and starts up a staircase. A large black shadow looms on the wall in the background. She halts, terrified, and hurries back towards camera, clutching her hand to her breast.

She walks along in profile, holding up her candle, then suddenly whips round again, terrified, as she hears another noise. She listens, looks up at the ceiling, then hurries off.

We see her again, her face gleaming white in the light of the candle, as she comes to the meeting point of several passages. She looks behind her again, takes a step forward and peers anxiously up a passage in the background.

> *In the complete silence, the girl suddenly heard her own heart . . . She heard her own heart, like pump-works, beating more and more loudly . . .*

Maria stands with her candle raised, looking away up the passage. A couple of skulls are mounted on the wall behind her. She hears another noise and whips round in alarm.

Seen in a longer shot, she is coming slowly and fearfully towards camera when suddenly a disembodied hand appears from the shadows just above her.

We see the candle held aloft in her hand. Rotwang's black and gleaming artificial hand slowly descends on the candle and grabs it, smothering the flame.

The hand snatches away the candle and withdraws into the shadows. Maria overcome with terror, runs backwards to the opposite wall.

She hurtles back against the wall and gazes round, clutching at her bosom, gnawing her fingers in panic. She jumps in terror as a brilliant circle of light from Rotwang's torch suddenly passes across her face. She looks off, following the beam with her eyes . . .

As it plays slowly over skulls and broken bones lying in niches in the wall.

Maria's face fills the screen; staring in terror, she mutters: *'Help!'*
She watches like a trapped animal as the torch beam plays across the floor, off-screen . . .

And comes to rest on a grotesque human skeleton lying on the rock-strewn floor.

Maria sees the skeleton and screams, pointing in horror.

> *Was it not as if a creature, such as the world had never seen: trunkless, nothing but arms, legs and head . . . but what a head! God—God in heaven! . . . was crouching on the floor before her, knees drawn up to chin, the damp arms supported right and left against the walls . . .*

Maria cowers back against the wall as the small, brilliant pool of light from Rotwang's torch advances slowly towards her across the floor. Like a disembodied presence, it reaches her feet and starts to travel up her body.

She gibbers with fear, turning her head from side to side as the torch beam travels slowly up her body, then shines full in her face. She stares, transfixed, her mouth open.

The torch beam shines straight into the camera; and behind are Rotwang's flowing grey hair and staring eyes.

Maria stares, mesmerized, tossing her head from side to side as the inventor begins to advance towards her off-screen. Suddenly she twists away and runs off.

> *With a shriek which tore her throat, the girl threw herself up, backwards—and then on and on, without looking round, pursued by the light which lashed her own shadow in springs before her feet—pursued by long, soft, feathery feet . . . by the icy breath which blew at her back.*

Now she comes scuttling up a sloping passageway towards us, Rotwang with his torch hurrying some way behind.

We see her again from below as the beam reaches out and catches her in mid-flight. She stands transfixed, cowering against the wall. The light whips across as she rushes to the opposite side of the passage, then slowly but surely drives her on up some steps.

Again she hurtles into the wall, raising a hand as if to ward off the pursuing beam. Again she rushes off . . .

And into a bricked-up archway. She stares down towards the torch again, gasps with horror, then continues her headlong flight, the beam of light still following without respite.

She reaches a dead end. The torch flickers on her back as she turns, falls forwards . . .

And lands against the wall, staring down into the light. Clutching her hands to her she screams violently: *'No! No! No! . . .'* and rushes off again.

We see her again, running off up a passage to the right.

> *She pressed her bleeding hands, right and left, against the stone wall, by the stone steps. She dragged herself up. She staggered up, step by step . . . There was the top.*

Seen from below, Maria hurtles on up the steps to Rotwang's house. There is a lighted opening in the background, at the top.

In the cellar in Rotwang's house, we see Maria run up the steps from the trap door and make for a door in the background.

> *The door was latchless. It had neither bolt or lock . . . In the gloomy wood glowed, copper-red, the seal of Solomon, the pentagram.*

Seen from behind, she tries the door frantically, but cannot open it. We follow her as she dashes across to another, beats her fists against it. The torch beam appears and fastens itself to her back. She freezes, then slowly, fearfully, begins to turn towards camera.

She saw a man at the edge of the trap-door and saw his smile . . .

In the background, Maria turns in the torch beam, while the sinister figure of Rotwang—dark robe, flowing grey hair—stands with his back to us at the top of the steps. They stare at one another for a long time.

Then it was as though she were extinguished, and she plunged into nothing . . .

Metropolis had the most saintly cathedral in the world, richly adorned with Gothic decoration. In times of which only the chronicles could tell, the star-crowned virgin on its tower used to smile, as a mother, from out her golden mantle, deep, deep down upon the pious red rooves, and the only companions of her graciousness were the doves which used to nest in the gargoyles of the water-spouts and the bells which were called after the four archangels and of which Saint Michael was the most magnificent.

In the dim interior of the great cathedral, figures kneel in prayer, all dressed in workers' overalls. Sculptured pillars gleam in the candle light. Freder appears in the background and wanders slowly forwards, looking from side to side.

The organ was thundering like the Trump of Doom. Singing from a thousand throats. Dies Irae . . . The incense clouded above the head of the multitude, which was kneeling before the eternal God.

Freder's head looks up and down, round and round, then stares up at something off-screen.

The darkly-clad worshippers get up and begin to file out around him, while Freder stands looking round in bewilderment. He walks forward to the left.

'*I sought Maria. Oh, I knew quite well that all the thousands could not hide her from me. If she were here I should find her out, as a bird finds its way to its nest. But my heart lay as if dead in my breast . . .*'

To one side of the church is a small recessed chapel. In the centre stands Death, with his great scythe and flowing cloak, an hour glass hanging at his girdle; while on either side, in niches, are statues of the Seven Deadly Sins. Freder appears in back view and walks slowly towards them.

TITLE : THE SEVEN DEADLY SINS.

Camera pans slowly round the curved recess, from left to right, then back again to hold on Death in the centre.
Freder stands gazing up at the figures off-screen. Slowly, he spreads his arms wide in an attitude of supplication.
Now seen in back view, he lets falls his arms and shakes his head hopelessly. Then he turns, comes towards us, and with a final glance at Death behind him, walks off in the foreground.

TITLE : MARIA WAS A PRISONER IN ROTWANG'S HOUSE.

Somewhere in the inventor's house, Maria backs along a gloomy corridor into a shaft of light cast by a window off-screen. Rotwang's dark figure suddenly appears in the foreground creeping after her.

They both pause, staring at one another.

A shot of girders and pillars, somewhere in the city. Freder, having come out of the church, shuffles hopelessly towards camera. Figures hurry to and fro in the background.

> *The roar of the streets wrapped itself, as a diver's helmet, about his ears. He walked on in his stupefaction, as though between thick glass walls. He had no thought apart from the name of his beloved, no consciousness apart from his longing for her.*

In Rotwang's house, Maria puts out a hand in panic as the inventor advances slowly towards her with crooked fingers.

She backs hurriedly along the wall, never taking her eyes off the inventor, off-screen.

The two of them are seen in profile as Rotwang makes a dash towards her. She grabs hold of a table which is standing just beside her, and swings it between the two of them. They stand glaring at one another. Rotwang speaks:

TITLE: 'COME, I AM GOING TO MAKE THE ROBOT LOOK LIKE YOU.'

We see the robot's sculptured metallic face, with its sightless pin-prick eyes.

Maria, cowering behind the table, gazes fearfully off at Rotwang.

Resume on the two of them in profile as he continues to speak. He shakes the table violently, trying to get at her. She holds on grimly.

We now see Rotwang's house from the outside—a blind wall with a single door bearing the pentagram in its centre, a steeply pitched tiled roof. The girders of some great modern construction loom on either side. Freder shuffles hopelessly towards us from the right.

Meanwhile, Rotwang finally manages to hurl the table aside, and grabs hold of Maria, forcing her back onto the table-top.

Seen from above, he grips her by the shoulders, forcing her down. She screams, tossing her head from side to side.

Rotwang's tangled mane of grey hair is seen in the centre of shot as she manages to force him back again.

Suddenly, she escapes from his grasp, leaps onto the table and grasps at the bars of a window in the roof above her head. Rotwang grabs hold of her from below.

We look down through the dirty glass of the window. Maria hangs on to the iron bars beneath, screaming as Rotwang tries to pull her down.

Another shot of the two of them from inside. She tries to beat him off with her arm, still hanging onto the bars with the other hand. Seen through the window again, she screams at the top of her voice. Freder, at that moment, is just walking past the house. He suddenly stops dead and spins round, looking upwards . . .

And, following his gaze, camera pans and tilts across the blind façade of Rotwang's house.

Freder gazes upwards, peering from side to side, trying to discover the source of the noise. He moves into close-up and cocks an ear, listening.

We see Maria's frantic face from above as she struggles and screams. Rotwang's face is dimly seen beneath her.

Freder suddenly recognizes the voice; he shouts: *'Maria!'* excitedly several times and cocks an ear again.

Maria, seen through the window, is still hanging onto the bars beneath. Rotwang has now nearly drawn himself up to her level, as she continues to scream . . .

While outside, Freder stands listening for all he's worth.

Now seen from behind, he stands for a moment before Rotwang's house. Then he dashes up to the door and beats his fists on it. He backs away and hurls himself against it again.

> *Copper-red, in the black wood of the door, glowed the seal of*
> *Solomon, the pentagram.*

Freder stands beating his fists against the door.

Meanwhile, Maria is still hanging from the bars, shouting and screaming, beating at Rotwang as he tries to haul her down.

Freder stands in back view, hammering furiously on the door.

> *He heard the echo of his drumming blows shake the house,*
> *as in dull laughter. But the copper Solomon's seal grinned*
> *at him from the unshaken door.*

Maria is seen again from above, screaming. Rotwang's gleaming artificial hand comes into view as he claps it over her mouth . . . And she drops into his arms in a dead faint.

Freder is still hammering at the door . . .

> *But in that same moment, the door opened noiselessly. It*
> *swung back in ghostly silence, leaving the way into the house*
> *absolutely free.*

71

. . . Freder stops and peers into the doorway. There is no one inside. A couple of luminous spirals hang from the ceiling.

We now see him from the inside, standing with his fists still clenched. He glances at the pentagram on the door, then comes slowly forward into the house, looking warily around.

Reverse shot from the outside as he walks into the hallway. Suddenly, the door slams shut.

Inside, Freder whips round and hurls himself against the door, trying to find a handle or lock. There is none. He turns and gazes in alarm towards camera . . .

Up some steps at the end of the corridor is another door. It swings slowly open, revealing a blank wall beyond.

Freder hurtles forward from the front door.

He runs up the corridor, in back view, and goes through the second doorway . . .

Which leads into Rotwang's study. Freder arrives just inside the door and looks off to the right . . .

Where he sees the top of a winding staircase leading down into the cellars beneath the house.

He looks across to the left . . .

And there an open doorway—flanked by bookcases laden with leather-bound tomes—leads into another room.

Freder runs off towards this door . . .

Which we see as he runs towards it in back view. Suddenly, he stops and turns . . .

As the door he came in through slams shut by itself.

Freder rushes back in the opposite direction again—and the door into the next room also slams behind him. He whips round at the noise, runs up to the door, beats his fists on it, but it remains firmly closed. He races off to the right . . .

And up to the door he came in through. He searches feverishly round the edges, looking for a lock. There is none. He turns, looks anxiously from side to side and finally rushes off again . . .

To the top of the staircase leading down into the cellar. There he halts, looks down, then back again, finally comes to a decision, and disappears down the steps.

As Freder reaches the bottom of the winding staircase which leads to the cellars, a door suddenly swings open in the background. He freezes, then steps towards it.

Seen from inside the door, he peers towards it, then comes forward again and picks up a long stick from a pile lying against the wall. He steps through the door, putting one foot against it to stop it slamming, and peers round into the room.

A reverse shot shows the cellar where the trap-door is situated. Camera pans in a circle, past the numerous doors, which are all closed.

> On the wood of each of these doors glowed, copper-red, the seal of Solomon, the pentagram.

Freder takes a step forward, almost forgets the door and turns with a start. He wedges his stick firmly in the doorway to stop the door from closing, then runs off to the left.

He runs up to one of the other doors and tries it. It remains shut. He looks round the room, then suddenly hears a noise off and whips round towards camera.

In the open doorway behind him, the stick suddenly snaps in half, and the door slams shut. Freder hurtles into view and throws himself against the door, trying feverishly to lever it open.

In a closer shot, he bangs his fists furiously against the wooden door. Finally he gives up and sinks exhausted against the door jamb. Suddenly, he notices something off-screen . . .

It is a piece of material caught beneath one of the doors. Freder's hand comes into view and snatches it up.

Freder picks up the material, looks at it, and recognises it as Maria's scarf. He looks round at the door, feverishly tries to find a way in, then puts his ear to it and listens, shouting and louder and more and more hysterically.

TITLE : 'MARIA !'

The scene changes to Rotwang's workshop; we are looking down on the head and naked shoulders of Maria, as she lies back in some kind of apparatus, her eyes closed, motionless. A metal helmet is fastened to her head with wires leading from terminals on it.

We now see Rotwang standing over Maria, who is lying on a table in the foreground, encased in a semi-cylindrical perspex cover fastened with metal bands. The apparatus is festooned with terminals and wires which lead to more terminals on the chair of the robot, seated in the background beneath the great pentagram on

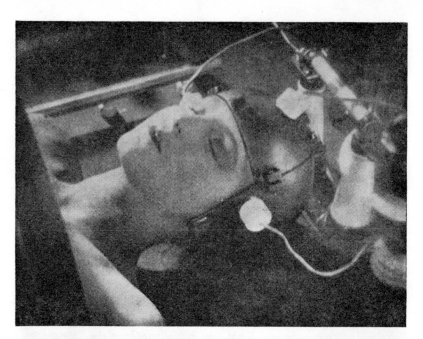

74

the wall. Rotwang walks to and fro, looks up, turns a handle, goes off to the left.

We now see the inventor's workshop from another angle. Maria is still in the foreground, while beyond her Rotwang walks across and inspects some thick white cables hanging from the ceiling. Beyond him is the transparent cylinder of bubbling liquid seen previously, whilst a furnace burns brightly in the background.

Rotwang goes over to a large transformer standing against the wall and throws a switch. Immediately the cylinder of liquid starts to bubble up, and turns a luminous white. Rotwang consults a chart on the wall, then walks towards camera.

We now see another part of the workshop. It is a fantastic maze of apparatus of all different kinds, with cables, terminals, dials on the wall. Rotwang walks across and throws another switch.

Elsewhere is a system of retorts linked by tubes and coiled cables, with a display screen in the middle; the cylinder of liquid bubbles merrily in the background.

Then we see, from above, a couple of relay switches mounted on terminals with white porcelain insulators.

Dissolve to a shot of a dark liquid bubbling in the bottom of a glass retort.

Dissolve again to a row of jars, with a bubbling white liquid inside them.

Rotwang stands surrounded by all this elaborate apparatus. He leaves the switch where he was previously, goes across to a squat grey box standing amidst his paraphernalia, and turns a handle on the front of it.

The white liquid bubbles in the jars.

Vertical neon tubes flash, near the bubbling retort.

Rotwang straightens up, reaches forward and throws another switch.

He comes towards camera, turns yet another switch.

On the display screen of the apparatus, surrounded by retorts, relays and cables, a diffuse white light appears and starts scanning in a circular motion.

Rotwang looks across to the other side of the workshop . . .

Where Maria lies encased in perspex, the cylinder of liquid now glowing a brilliant white in the background, A large glass globe hanging from the ceiling begins to glow brilliantly.

Rotwang starts forward, stares intently at the spectacle off-screen, then with a decisive gesture suddenly throws two more switches. With mad, staring eyes, he glares straight towards camera.

Resume on Maria in the apparatus. Two massive electric arcs leap from either end of the perspex casing to the globe in the ceiling, flickering and crackling with increasing intensity.

With an air of feverish activity, Rotwang turns and throws a couple more switches behind him, then adjusts a handle in front of him. We now see the robot, seated on its throne, with cables and connectors leading to Maria off-screen. Suddenly a couple of horizontal rings of light appear round the throne and begin to move up and down in contrary directions, crossing over one another and glowing brighter and brighter.

On the apparatus, the arcs from the ceiling glow brighter and begin to play to and fro along the perspex case.

The robot is now surrounded by four rings of light, two hovering at the top and bottom of the throne, two more moving up and down in the middle.

Rotwang throws another switch . . .

While the dark liquid bubbles in the retort.

Rotwang turns to and fro, adjusting his controls . . .

And the bubbling retort is seen reflected in the seething cylinder of liquid.

Dissolve to the moving relays, their contacts arcing as the current passes. The bubbling retort dissolves in over them . . .

And Rotwang throws another switch with a quick, decisive gesture. We now look right across the workshop from a low angle. Maria lies in the perspex casing in the foreground, while in the background the robot is seated on her throne, seeming from this angle to be suspended over the apparatus. Numerous concentric rings of light pass up and down her body while the electric arcs flash and glow between her and Maria.

A series of dissolves shows:

The bubbling cylinder of liquid/The retort./The white light scanning the display screen./The retort again more clearly, with the bubbling liquid in superimposition.

Rotwang, at his control panel, snatches up a gauge attached to a long rubber tube; he looks at it and turns another switch.

Meanwhile the retort keeps bubbling, and light gleams brilliantly from the cylinder of liquid in the background.

Rotwang puts down the gauge and snatches up two more wand-like devices with gradations at one end, also attached to rubber tubes. He starts throwing switches on the wall in a rapid sequence.

The lightning continues to play to and fro across the recumbent figure of Maria, while the cylinder of liquid seethes and bubbles beyond.

The inventor tosses aside his gauges and continues throwing switches more and more feverishly.

We see the robot again, wreathed in moving bands of light. There is now a glowing area right in the centre of its chest, with a light flashing on and off like a pulsing heart.

The electric arcs continue to flash and play over the apparatus containing Maria, while the cylinder of liquid bubbles in the background.

A close-up shows the bubbling liquid with foam on the top.

The rings round the robot are different sizes now; they pass rapidly up and down while the light flashes in its chest.

Rotwang reaches out behind him and pulls a large lever . . .
And a glowing circulatory system begins to appear on the robot's
body, the heart pulsing in the centre.
The rings of light play up and down across the robot's face, while
the arcs flash intermittently, obscuring it from view. Suddenly it
dissolves away, to be replaced by the head of Maria, eyes closed,
still wearing the robot's helmet. The rings of light fade out and
the robot Maria opens her eyes and gazes straight at the camera.
Beneath the perspex cover, the real Maria's eyes are closed. Her
head drops slowly onto her shoulder . . .
While the robot looks at us with a harsh, brazen gaze.

We return to Freder in the cellar, sitting dejectedly against the door
with Maria's scarf in his hands. He looks up suddenly and starts
forward . . .
As the door opposite him slowly swings open.
Freder leaps up . . .
He rushes out of the door, in back view, and starts up the stairs.
We next see him arriving at the top of the spiral staircase in the

room adjoining Rotwang's workshop. The long black curtains hiding the robot's throne are in the background. While Freder stands looking around him, Rotwang comes through the curtains, drawing them to behind him. Freder turns and sees Rotwang; looking grim he hurries across to the inventor and angrily holds Maria's scarf under his nose.

Title: 'Where is Maria?'

He speaks accusingly, pointing downwards to the cellars.
The two men face one another as Freder continues to speak angrily, waving the scarf at Rotwang. The inventor looks down his nose as he replies.

Title: 'She is with your father.'

The robot is standing just inside the great swing doors of Fredersen's office. She is a parody of the real Maria, her face subtly twisted into a cruel, provocative expression.
Fredersen stands staring off at her. He tells her to come forward . . .
And the robot swings slowly forwards, almost filling the screen.
We look in through the open front door of Rotwang's house. The glowing spirals hang on either side. Rotwang follows Freder to the door and leans against the doorpost, watching as he stumbles away.
Back in the great office, the Master of Metropolis and the parody of Maria stand gazing into one another's eyes. With the same provocative expression, the robot leans very slowly towards him.
Fredersen stares intently at her; he speaks:

Title: 'The copy is perfect. Now go down to the workers and undo Maria's teaching; stir them up to criminal acts.'

Seen from his viewpoint, the robot gazes into Fredersen's eyes, and very slowly winks. Then she nods her head.
We see the two of them in profile as the robot stares into Fredersen's eyes, stretching out her neck towards him. Slowly, he raises his hands and rests them on her shoulders . . .
And at that moment, Freder wrenches open the swing doors and rushes into the room. He suddenly stops, transfixed by what he sees.
   In the middle of the room, which was filled with a cutting brightness, stood John Fredersen, holding a woman in his

arms. And the woman was Maria. She was not struggling. Leaning far back in the man's arms, she was offering him her mouth, her alluring mouth, that deadly laugh . . .

The couple are standing by Fredersen's vast curved desk with its dials and push-buttons. Fredersen looks up and sees his son off-screen. The parody of Maria slowly turns her head . . .

And Freder starts back, throwing up his hands.

Great flashing discs of light move towards camera, as if blinding him.

He passes a hand over his eyes, trying to drive away the hallucination.

Fredersen and the robot are almost in one another's arms. She is staring off at Freder with a sinister and provocative expression. The picture wavers, becomes hazy . . .

He did not see his father. He saw only the girl—no, neither did he see the girl, only her mouth and sweet, wicked laugh.

Freder leans forward, arms outstretched, eyes staring, as he shouts out :

TITLE : 'MARIA.'

He sees the robot and his father, standing arm in arm, surrounded by whirling images of the great city.

Seen in front of the great swing doors, he throws his head back and shields his eyes . . .

As flashing discs and stars of light come straight at him.

Sunbursts flash around Freder as he waves his hands wildly, covering his eyes. He staggers, trying to keep his balance . . .

As the montage of images whirls round the couple.

Freder staggers again, clutching his hands to his head, and the floor begins to lurch and pulsate beneath him like a stormy sea.

The robot, the parody of Maria, stares at him with her alluring expression, a montage of eyes whirling round her.

He sees more flashing discs of light . . .

His father's face, staring at him sternly . . .

The robot's brazen gaze, her black-rimmed eyes . . .

Rotwang leaning forward, eyes bulging, mouth open to show his crooked teeth. Scythe-like gashes of light appear all round the inventor. The light effect continues as Freder's vision changes to . . .

The figure of Death—a hideous skull with half its teeth missing, holding a human thigh bone in its hands . . .

Then back to the brazen gaze of the robot, with other faces whirling round in superimposition . . .

And finally nothing but a mass of whirling, curving streaks of light. We see Freder lurching drunkenly in front of the great swing doors. The streaks of light become sunbursts. They continue while Freder disappears, and discs of light zoom towards camera.

Freder sinks to the ground with an agonized cry, his hands clawing the air. Light effects like falling rain surround him.

The luminous shower continues while Freder disappears. Sunbursts shoot up in darkness, then whorls and discs of light.

We see Freder with his arms outstretched—falling, falling, through streaks and discs of light, through light effects like shock waves, faster and faster. Suddenly he disappears. The light effects continue, then fade to black.

The scene changes to a bedroom in the Fredersen residence where Freder is lying back in a luxurious bed, his head resting on elaborately embroidered pillows. Electric lamps glow softly on either side of the bed. Freder's eyes are closed and there is a tortured expression on his face.

Freder's head, in profile, moves uneasily on the pillows, while a nurse moves around in the background, preparing some medicine. A man appears in the foreground in evening dress, puts down a top hat on the bedside table and leans over the reclining figure. It is Fredersen. He puts his hands on his son's shoulders and looks down at him with the greatest concern. He runs a hand gently over his face, sighs and straightens up again, then picks up his top hat and goes off.

In the corridor outside—decorated with curving Twenties designs— Fredersen speaks to a tall, dark manservant in a frock coat and a shorter, grey-haired butler just behind him. Then he turns and goes out, followed by the manservant, whose name is Slim. The butler closes the door on them.

Meanwhile Freder, seen slightly from above, raises his head painfully from the pillows and reaches out towards a card which Fredersen has left on the bedside table.

His hand clutches at the card.

Slowly and painfully, Freder raises the card so that he can read it. Close-up of the card in his hand. It is a printed invitation which reads: 'C.A. ROTWANG INVITES MR. JOHN FREDERSEN TO BE HIS GUEST THIS EVENING.'

The scene dissolves to a great room hung with curtains and drapes, somewhere in Metropolis . . .

> *Strangely enough no one knew the house. Nobody could remember ever having entered it, or having known anything of its occupants. One turned up at ten. One was well dressed. One entered the house and found a big party . . . It was an odd thing that all the people collected there seeming to be waiting for something, of which they did not know . . .*

. . . As the scene opens, camera tracks and pans across the room from a high angle, showing groups of guests standing around chatting. They are all male, all in evening dress.

We look over the heads of the guests as they stand around, talking, obviously waiting for something to happen.

In another shot, the camera tracks sideways amongst the guests. We now see Fredersen and Rotwang standing in front of the curtains, dressed in tail coats and white ties. Fredersen turns to the inventor and asks him a question. In answer, he raises his artificial hand and points dramatically off-screen.

TITLE: 'NOW WE SHALL SEE WHETHER PEOPLE BELIEVE THE ROBOT IS A CREATURE OF FLESH AND BLOOD.'

A couple of middle-aged guests stand chatting. One of them brushes a speck of dirt from his immaculate evening suit.

We see two more guests chatting amiably to one another.

Another group is seen from above, one man holding forth. Another man, with his back to us, lays his hand on the speaker's arm. They all pause and turn slowly, looking off towards the right . . .

Where a strange and exotic spectacle meets their eyes. On a platform surrounded by drapes at one end of the room stands a vast ornamental urn, with decorative panels in relief round the side and a dome-shaped openwork top. Supporting it on their shoulders are the kneeling figures of half-naked Nubian slaves, with large gold earrings. A luminous glow is seen from inside the domed top, whence clouds of steam rise lazily upwards.

The guests all look round.

We now see the urn at bottom of frame, surrounded by drapes reaching up to the ceiling. Slowly, of its own accord, the great domed cover rises up towards us.

One of the second pair of guests seen chatting earlier breaks off and grips his companion by the arm, staring off to the left.

Resume on the urn. The domed cover opens completely towards camera, like a great oyster about to reveal a precious pearl, and the figure of the robot, the parody of Maria, rises slowly from inside amid clouds of steam.

Close-up of the circular hole in the centre of the cover. The robot's head rises into view, so that the metal top radiates like a sun around her. Her eyes are cast down and she is wearing a brilliant, shimmering metallic robe with a fan-shaped head-dress of similar material. The two guests seen previously start forward, as does everyone else around them.

A longer shot of the great ornamental cover of the urn. Steam wafts slowly round the motionless figure of the robot, then the cover fades away leaving her standing alone in her flowing, shim-

mering robe, brilliantly lit against the dark background of the drapes.

Several of the guests lean forward, their eyes riveted on the spectacle.

> *Over her shoulders, her breasts, her lips, her knees, there ran an incessant, a barely perceptible trembling. It was no frightened trembling. It was like the trembling of the final spinal fins of a luminous, deep sea fish.*

The robot is seen from below, brilliantly lit from in front. Slowly she raises her hands from her side in the pose of an oriental goddess. The lights go out and she is now lit from behind, silhouetted half naked through the transparent material of her flowing robe. Holding her arms out from her sides, she begins to turn slowly, with a slightly mechanical movement.

Three more guests stare in amazement . . .

While the robot turns, back to camera, now beginning to rotate her hips in an unmistakably sexual motion. Her robe and head-dress shimmer in the light from behind.

The guests lean forward, transfixed, their expressions turning slowly from amazement to lust.

85

No dance, no scream, no cry of an animal in heat could have
so lashing an effect as the trembling of this shimmering body,
which seemed, in its calm, in its solitude, to impart the waves
of its incitement to every soul in the room.

The robot Maria turns to face camera again, arms outstretched,
rotating her hips like a belly dancer.

Now she is seen from below, her robe a brilliant, shimmering film
around her half-naked body.

We return to Freder, who is lying back in bed with his eyes closed.
The nurse leans across and mops his forehead, then draws the
blankets up over him.

On the other side of the room, the old butler picks up Freder's
workman's overalls and heavy shoes from a chair beside the door
and reaches for the door handle. As he does so one of the shoes
falls to the floor with a bang.

Freder leaps up in bed at the noise and leans forward, staring
straight at camera.

A closer shot of him leaning forward, staring upwards in a mixture
of horror and amazement.

Back to the robot Maria, brilliantly lit against the dark background of the drapes. She has now taken off her flimsy robe and whirls round and round holding it up in her arms, displaying her almost naked breasts. A long skirt of thin translucent strands radiates from a jewelled belt at her waist.

The guests lean forward, eyes goggling at the spectacle before them . . .

While the robot continues to whirl round and round. Suddenly, she lets go of the flying robe . . .

And kneels on the platform, rotating her naked torso and arms.

Seen from below, she dances, kicking up her legs.

A closer shot as she wiggles her hips, turning her head from side to side.

We now see the guests from above, leaning forward, slavering, superimposed over a shot of enormous eyes. The guests fade out and we are left with a montage of their eyes, like some grotesque monster, gazing lustfully towards camera.

The robot dances up and down, arms outstretched, her head and shoulders seen from below.

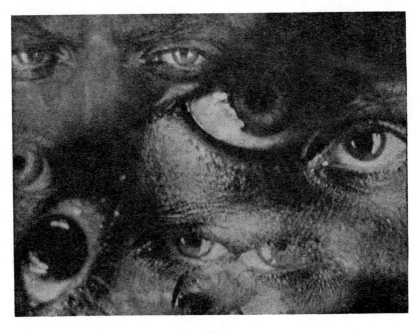

The goggling eyes blink . . .

And the robot dances, back to camera.

The eyes gape . . .

And she dances facing camera.

We see one enormous goggling eye . . .

While she dances wildly, arms outspread, gazing down at the guests off-screen.

Freder meanwhile is sitting up in bed, staring at this wild vision.

The robot dances wildly, legs apart, looking down at the guests with an expression of lustful joy.

Freder stares wildly as the nurse's hands come into view from the left. She puts one hand behind his head and makes him drink from a glass. His eyes close for a moment and the nurse goes off. He is about to sink back again when he starts forward once more as he sees . . .

The robot Maria rising from the floor against the darkened drapes, seated on a grotesque, writhing, many-headed sea-monster. One jewelled hand is crooked in front of her, the other holds a goblet aloft, like a Bacchante.

Close-up of Freder, staring and staring . . .

While the vision rises up towards the ceiling.

Freder stares in awe and horror . . .

As the robot continues to rise slowly upwards. We now see that her grotesque steed is mounted on the great ornamental urn, supported not by the negro slaves but by the figures of the Seven Deadly Sins from the cathedral.

Freder stares, shuddering in horror. The nurse has turned out the light and he is in darkness.

Resume on the spectacle as the robot rises further. She throws both hands in the air and from the bottom of the frame the guests rush up, stretching out towards her, forming a sea of hands around the great urn.

As Freder continues to stare into the darkness, his vision changes . . .

We are in the cathedral; we see the figure of Death and the Seven Deadly Sins in their niches, dimly lit with darkness all around. Suddenly Death begins to move, raising the human thigh bone in his hands and putting it to his mouth.

And through the silence which did not dare to breathe, rang

the sound of a flute. Death was playing. The minstrel was playing the song which nobody plays after him, on his flute which was a human bone.

Seen from below, Death plays on the thigh bone with crooked fingers.

In a general shot of the scene, the figures of the Seven Deadly Sins step forward jerkily from their niches on either side.

Death plays his thigh-bone flute . . .

And the Seven Deadly Sins continue to jerk forward.

We see Freder staring in horror in the gloom of his room, then return to the cathedral . . .

The ghostly minstrel stepped out from his side-niche, carved in wood, in hat and wide cloak, scythe on shoulder, the hour-glass dangling from his girdle.

. . . With a jerky step, playing on his thigh-bone flute, Death comes slowly towards camera.

Outside in the city of Metropolis, steam blasts from the great sirens, signalling the end of a shift. Windows shine brilliantly in a cliff-like building beyond.

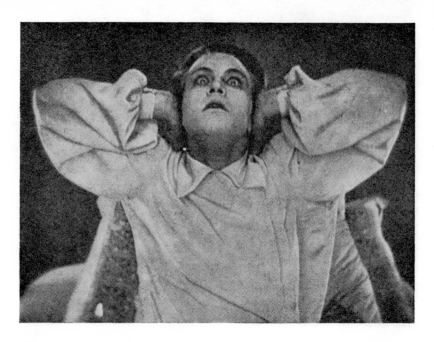

We return to Freder, now in light again. He starts and claps his hands over his ears as the steam-whistles sound off-screen.

Seen from below, the grotesque figure of Death advances slowly down the aisle of the cathedral. There is a great rose window high in the wall beyond him. He steps forward, sweeping his scythe with great swinging strokes; the wheeling scythe becomes a flash of light . . .

> Death swung his scythe and made a whistling cut. The earth
> and all the stars quivered . . . Blue sparks flew out of the
> steel. Then Death made a second blow. A rain of stars poured
> down from the sky.
> Death nodded with satisfaction and set off, on his way through
> the great Metropolis.

Freder starts back in his bed, throwing up an arm as a curved flash of light like the scythe of Death passes across in front of him. Shouting in horror, he sinks back onto the pillows. Fade out.

The scene changes to the gloomy corridor in Rotwang's house which we have seen previously. A shaft of light falls from the window in the ceiling onto the table beneath. Maria sits hunched forward on a chair beside it while Rotwang sits in profile on the left, gesturing with his artificial hand as he says:

TITLE: 'JOHN FREDERSEN IS LOOKING FOR AN EXCUSE TO USE VIOLENCE AGAINST THE WORKERS.'

As Rotwang continues to talk, Maria turns away from him in despair, claps her hands over her ears and flops forward helplessly on the table. Rotwang leans towards her inert figure, talking and pleading.

TITLE: 'MARIA, YOU ALWAYS PLEADED FOR PEACE—BUT NOW THE ROBOT IN YOUR LIKENESS HAS BEEN COMMANDED TO INCITE THE WORKERS TO VIOLENCE.'

Rotwang leans towards Maria, fingers crooked, talking persuasively. She shrinks away from him, in back view in the foreground.
Seen in reverse shot, she crosses her hands on her chest; Rotwang's crooked hands are on the table in the foreground, one of them black and gleaming.
Rotwang leans forward, still talking, his hands outstretched like claws on the table.
He is seen in back view as Maria shrinks away from him, turning her head from side to side as if to avoid hearing what he says.

TITLE: THE WORKERS ACCEPTED THE ROBOT AS MARIA.

A vault, like the vault of a sepulchre—human heads so closely crowded as to produce the effect of clods of a freshly ploughed field. All faces turned to one point: to the source of a light, as mild as God. Candles burnt with sword-like flames. Slender, lustrous swords of light stood in a circle around the head of a girl . . .

We are back in the cavern in the catacombs beneath Metropolis. Now, instead of the real Maria, it is her robot counterfeit who stands before the altar, haranguing the workers with a fierce gleam in her eye.
We look across the cavern; in front of us the workers stand or kneel, facing the altar in the background, listening intently.

TITLE: 'I HAVE PREACHED PATIENCE—'

91

Seen from the side, the robot leans forward, holding out her hands. *The voice came from out the blood-red mouth. It was like a flame, hot and pointed. It was full of wicked sweetness.*
Resume on the scene; the workers all lean forward as she continues to speak in the background.
Seen from below, she suddenly turns and glares off towards the left . . .
While the ranks of workers lean forwards, listening avidly to her words.
Camera pans left as she turns to another part of the cavern, flinging out her arms.
Some of the workers crowd round a large tombstone while she leans towards them from the background, arms outstretched.

TITLE: 'BUT YOUR MEDIATOR HAS NOT COME—AND WILL NEVER COME.'

We move to a luxuriously furnished sitting room in the residence of the Master of Metropolis. Freder is reclining in a deeply upholstered armchair, beside which is a table bearing decanters and a half empty glass. Light filters through net curtains from a window in the background. Freder leans forward with a sigh and looks down at a book which he is holding in his hand.
Shot of the door, with an elaborately painted motif on it. It flies open and Joseph, the dismissed secretary, rushes in, eyes wide, dressed in worker's overalls. He stretches out a hand, calling to Freder off-screen.
Freder whips round, looking up from his book . . .
While Joseph shuts the door carefully behind him and listens for sounds of pursuit.
Freder starts to his feet and rushes off towards the door . . .
Where he and Joseph throw themselves into one another's arms. They converse rapidly, overjoyed to see one another, then Freder steps back and looks his friend up and down, noticing his overalls. Joseph nods and says:

TITLE: 'MARIA IS INCITING THE WORKERS TO REVOLT.'

They are seen standing in the middle of the ornately decorated sitting room; there are two thickly upholstered armchairs in the foreground. Freder is horror-struck at the news and comes towards camera, sinking down in one of the armchairs. Joseph stands over him as he adds:

TITLE: 'SHE HAS TOLD THEM TO DESTROY EVERYTHING.'

As Joseph finishes speaking, Freder leaps to his feet, gazing at him in amazement. He grips him by the arm and says:

TITLE: 'I CANNOT BELIEVE IT.'

Freder hurries out through a doorway at the end of the room and turns on a light in the next room, while Joseph goes and listens again at the door he came in by. Freder reappears, slinging a dark cloak around his shoulders, and the two men hurry out.

We return to the cavern, where the robot Maria is seen from below, violently haranguing the workers off-screen. Camera pans as she moves across in front of the altar.
We look down on the workers in the cavern. They start to move restlessly and get up and crowd forward, listening intently . . .
As she pours out a torrent of words.

> But no peace proceeded from out these words. Little red snakes hissed through the air. The air was hot—and agony to breathe . . .

The robot stands in front of the altar, while the workers lean forward, excitedly beating their chests.

> Dark angry waves were the heads before her. These waves frothed, raged and roared. Here and there a hand shot up in the air.

Seen from the side, the workers lean forward eagerly, looking over one another's shoulders.
Others lean forward with glaring eyes and twisted, angry expressions.

> Words sprang up, foam flecks of the surf. But the voice of the girl was like a tongue of fire, drawing enticing, burning above the heads.

Standing in front of the altar, the robot beats the air with her fist.

TITLE: 'YOU HAVE WAITED PATIENTLY TOO LONG. THE TIME HAS COME TO ACT!'

And the workers all surge forward, waving their fists in the air.

Seen in close-up, the robot looks from side to side, glaring at the workers from her black-rimmed eyes, words pouring in a torrent from her vampire mouth.

Title : 'Why should you sweat yourselves to death to benefit the lord of Metropolis ?'

Seen from above, several workers gaze off towards the robot. One of them starts forward, beating his chest and crying out.
More workers lean forward, in three-quarter back view. The robot suddenly appears from the left, leaning across a great block of stone, as she asks :

Title : 'Who keeps the machines going ?'

Frenziedly they shout : *'Us, us!'*
Seen from above, more workers lean towards us. With glaring eyes, they shout : *'Us, us!'*, beating their chests with their fists.
Meanwhile, Freder and Joseph are hurriedly descending the candle-lit staircase which leads down into the cavern. Joseph breathlessly explains the situation as they come towards us.
We now see the bottom of the staircase; in the foreground the workers lean forward, shouting and beating their fists on their chests. The figures of the two men appear, coming down the steps, and pause.
Freder stands, staring forward, with Joseph a little way behind him. Reverse shot of the spectacle which meets his eyes. In the background, over a sea of workers' head, is the candle-lit altar, flanked by two great stone plinths. The robot is leaning across one of these, face to face with a group of workers. They all shout and beat their chests. She runs across to the other plinth . . .
And leans over it, staring into the contorted faces of the workers as she asks :

Title : 'Who are the slaves of the machines ?'

The workers lean towards her in the foreground, their faces grotesque and twisted as they shout : *'Us, us!'*
Shot of more workers leaning forward, shouting in their turn.
The robot is seen in close-up. She looks from side to side, then straight at camera, clenching her fists as she rants on . . .

And still the workers lean forward, shouting with fanatical expressions.

Wild with fury, the robot shouts:

TITLE: 'LET THE MACHINES STOP!'

We look over the workers' heads toward the robot Maria. The workers raise their fists and wave them in the air, shouting wildly. Then they all surge forward as the robot leaps onto one of the plinths.

She throws her arms in the air as she shouts:

TITLE: 'DESTROY THE MACHINES!'

And scythes the air with her arms.

She is seen again on the plinth in the background, above a forest of upraised fists. A worker climbs up and crouches on the plinth in front of her.

A voice shouted from among the multitude: 'Lead us on, Maria!' A mighty wave—all the heads broke forward . . .

A sea of white faces, they surge forward in the gloom, waving their fists in the air.

Seen in close-up, the robot tosses her head and shouts wildly.

While the workers, seen from above, surge forward with contorted faces.

Meanwhile, Freder and Joseph are still standing on the steps in the background, horrified by the scene they are witnessing. Joseph has his arm round Freder, whose cloak has nearly slipped from his shoulders, revealing his white silk garments underneath.

The robot is gazing down at the workers with a smile of evil satisfaction on her face. She jerks her head up and gazes straight at camera.

> *The blood red mouth of the girl laughed and flamed. The eyes above it flamed, huge and greenish black . . . Over her shoulders, her breasts, her hips, her knees, there ran an incessant, a barely perceptible trembling.*

Resume on the two men in the background. Joseph restrains Freder, who is trying to leap forward in a vain effort to stop the proceedings.

> *The multitude moaned. The multitude gasped. The multitude stretched out its hands.*

The workers at the bottom of the steps leap forward, faces contorted, shouting and waving their fists. In the background Freder finally frees himself from Joseph and runs down the steps after them.

He leans forward, pointing an accusing finger, while Joseph looks on behind.

> *A voice shouted out, sobbing with rage and pain:*

TITLE: 'YOU ARE NOT MARIA!'

The robot is seen from below, surrounded by workers' faces, with the man kneeling on the plinth in front of her. They all look up at the sound of Freder's voice.

> *The multitude turned around. The multitude saw a man standing in the background of the arch . . . The man was more ghastly to see than one who has bled to death.*

The workers just in front of Freder look round as he comes down several more steps, leaning forward, pointing and shouting.

Freder shouts again, with Joseph behind him . . .

96

While the workers look in bewilderment from Freder to the robot off-screen.

Brilliantly lit in the candle-light, the robot stands gazing towards Freder, an expression of total perversity on her face.

More workers stand looking to and fro, shuffling around, bewildered by this new turn of events.

Freder is seen in long shot, standing at the bottom of the steps in his white silk clothes, one arm raised in an accusing gesture. The workers milling in front of him turn towards the robot . . .

As do the workers standing just beneath her.

With Joseph standing just behind him, Freder turns from side to side, feverishly addressing the workers around him.

TITLE : 'MARIA PLEADS FOR PEACE, NOT FOR VIOLENCE. THIS IS NOT MARIA!'

The robot laughs perversely.

Then a low angle shot includes the workers in front of her. They all gaze off towards Freder, then the man crouching on the plinth suddenly throws up an arm and shouts :

TITLE : 'JOHN FREDERSEN'S SON!'

The workers all surge towards Freder, waving their fists in the air. He throws up his arms.

In a closer shot of the scene, the workers threaten Freder, who stands with his arms raised, while Joseph tries to fend them off.

Resume on the workers round the robot; the man crouching on the plinth sweeps his fists through the air and yells :

TITLE : 'KILL HIM!'

The multitude shouted. The multitude hurled itself around. The multitude made to lay hold of the son of John Fredersen.

Seen from above the workers surge towards the two men, shouting and waving their fists. Freder and Joseph fight them off wildly.

Freder stands with fists flailing, fighting for his life.

We see Joseph, doing likewise . . .

Then resume on Freder.

Joseph is seen in three-quarter back view, fighting off the workers. More workers surge forward in the background as Freder grapples with a man in front of him.

97

Now he stands pressed back against the wall. He throws the man aside and takes on several more.

More workers surge forward, shouting and waving their fists.

We resume on the scene around the altar. The man crouched at the robot's feet leaps down from his perch and shouts at the workers around him, holding up his arms:

TITLE : 'LET NO MAN REMAIN BEHIND, WE ARE DESTROYING THE MACHINES !'

The workers round the robot all shout and wave their fists in the air. One of them seizes her round the legs and carries her bodily from the plinth, while she throws her arms wide in a gesture of triumph.

> *The multitude left him alone and raced on. On the shoulders of the multitude the girl was dancing and singing. She sang with her blood-red mouth of deadly sin!*

Camera tracks out in front of the robot as she is carried triumphantly forward by the cheering workers, her arms spread wide.

> *Like the rush of a thousand wings the step of the multitude thundered through the narrow passages of the City of the Dead . . .*

We move to the great square in the middle of the workers' city, lighted tenements looming on either side. In the centre of the square, the robot stands on the platform on which the great gong is mounted, while a man throws a lever to operate the alarm. The workers surge around platform, waving their arms in the air.

The robot is seen in close-up, a triumphant expression on her face. She jerks her head from side to side in a mechanical movement, looking down at the workers off-screen.

We look down from above into one of the streets in the workers' city. More workers and their drably dressed women stream out of the tenement blocks and race towards the square.

On the platform, the workers' self-appointed leader is now organizing the crowd with shouts and gestures, while the robot moves jerkily by the gong in the background.

Again we look down on the street as the approaching workers come to a halt, crowding round and looking off into the square.

By the gong, the robot Maria looks down at the workers with a

perverse expression . . .

While the workers' leader stands in back view, shouting and rousing the crowd to action. They stand below him, a sea of upturned faces, raising their arms in the air.

Close-up of a worker shouting, a fanatical gleam in his eye. Fists wave in the foreground, while in the background the man operating the alarm looks up in fascination at the robot . . .

And she, with a triumphant expression, shouts to the crowd beneath her, gesticulating wildly.

Finally, she leaps down from the platform and rushes towards camera, followed by the workers and their women.

Seen from above, she rushes through the crowd, who all begin to surge after her.

> *The girl danced along before the streaming, bawling multitude. She led the multitude on. She led the tramping multitude forward against the heart of the machine city of Metropolis.*

We look up a flight of steps towards the great passenger lifts which lead to the machine rooms. The robot Maria runs up the steps and the crowd surge after her, almost filling the screen.

We are now looking directly down through the glass roof of one of the lifts. The robot runs into the lift cage, turns and waves on the workers, who crowd in after her.

More workers crowd forward, waving their fists and shouting . . . While the mob continues to surge up the steps towards the lift entrance.

Seen over rows of workers' heads, the robot stands on the edge of the first lift cage, now crammed full, and shouts down to the mob in the foreground.

More workers enter another empty lift, moving away from camera. And all along the line, the workers rush forward, into the waiting lifts.

Seen from below, the first lift cage now rises up, bearing the robot and its load of workers. They shout wildly, waving down at the rest of the workers waiting their turn below.

Seen from the side, another rushing torrent of workers streams into the lifts.

They crowd forward into one of the cages . . .

While in another a worker rushes up to the control panel at the side and beckons his fellows in after him.

We resume on the first lift as it rises slowly upwards—the robot standing with legs and arms spread at the front—and finally disappears up the shaft past a notice saying '326'.

More workers crowd into a lift, a man at the controls in the foreground.

We look down on another cage as it fills up. In the background more workers struggle to climb in, but their colleagues motion them away, pointing to the next lift along.

Another cage is seen from below, disappearing up the shaft past a notice saying '125'. The workers lean through the bars of the cage, waving their hands, faces contorted, like animals in a zoo.

The scene changes to the long tiled corridor leading to the machine rooms, with the great iron gates at one end. Led by the robot, the workers stream into view from the foreground.

We look through the gates as the workers run up outside.

Still seen from inside, the robot and the workers struggle frenziedly, trying to force apart the steel bars.

In a longer shot from inside, more workers rush up. The robot beckons on several with sledgehammers, and they start attacking the bars on the left, while others climb up the gates on the right.

In the workers' city below, the workers are still swarming into one of the overloaded lift cages, more of their colleagues waiting in the foreground.

We look up over a forest of workers' heads. They all wave wildly as one of the lift cages goes slowly up the shaft, a worker hanging from the bars on the outside.

More workers are helped into another cage by their comrades . . . While far above, in the corridor, the workers are attacking the steel bars with sledgehammers, cheered on by the robot and their mates. The lift in shaft '125' starts on another journey, its occupants leaning and shouting through the bars . . .

While the remaining workers and women leave the square and rush towards the lifts off-screen.

They reach one of the entrances, and pile into the lift. The barrier rises in front of them.

TITLE : NOT ONE MAN OR WOMAN REMAINED BEHIND.

We move to the lighted entrance of one of the tenement houses, now deserted, with boards carrying the inhabitants' identification numbers on either side. Suddenly a small boy appears on the staircase, his arm round a little girl.

Back in the corridor leading to the machine rooms, the crowd of workers are seen from inside the iron gates, still hammering and levering away at the bars.

Finally they force the bars aside and the robot runs through, urging the others after her.

A longer shot of the scene : one side of the gate is breached. The robot rushes off to the right and the others stream after her.

We now move to the interior of the great machine room, with girders rising from concrete foundations and workers jerking mechanically at their control panels on either side. The robot rushes towards camera, followed by the milling crowd of workers. Some of them run up and haul their mates off the control panels, while the robot points and runs off to the left. They all follow.

TITLE : 'TO THE CENTRAL POWERHOUSE !'

The heart of the machine city of Metropolis dwelt in a white, cathedral-like building. The heart of the machine city of

101

Metropolis was guarded by one single man. The man's name was Grot, and he loved his machine.

In the office of the Master of Metropolis, we see a large tickertape apparatus hanging from the wall by the door. Fredersen comes in, inspects the tape, then turns a dial on the apparatus.

Seen from behind, he turns another dial. The figures HM2 appear on an illuminated screen in front of him. Then a series of pictures from the central power house appear beneath. Fredersen adjusts the picture to 'hold' as the image of Grot, the chief engineer, appears by a control panel, rushing nervously to and fro. Fredersen picks up a telephone receiver from the machine beside him and presses a button.

We now see the massive, bearded Grot directly, pacing nervously across the floor of the power house, hands thrust in his pockets. He whips round as he hears a noise from an identical machine to the one in Fredersen's office, on the wall behind him.

Resume on Fredersen. In the picture on the screen in front of him, Grot rushes up and picks up a receiver; he speaks agitatedly into the phone, his eyes bulging.

Title : 'The workers are destroying the machines.'

Fredersen, in profile, talks urgently into the phone.
While Grot at his end continues:

Title : 'What shall I do?'

Resume on Fredersen, three-quarters back to camera, with Grot on the screen in front of him. Grot continues:

Title : 'If they destroy the power house, the workers' city will be flooded.'

Fredersen's eyes bulge as he suddenly shouts, shaking his fist.

Title : 'Open the doors.'

Resume on him at the screen. At the other end, Grot is shouting into the telephone in disbelief. Fredersen hangs up without another word and cuts the picture.

By now the workers are streaming into the power house, coming down a wide flight of steps towards camera, shouting and waving their arms.

In front of his control panel with its dials and flashing lights, Grot lumbers forward threateningly, brandishing a vast spanner and bellowing at the workers.

More workers come pouring down the steps; they halt in the foreground, looking up at Grot.

He shouts at them, waving his arms . . .

While the workers stream on down the steps, the robot in their midst urging them on.

Grot leans forward, shouting angrily:

TITLE: 'HAVE YOU GONE MAD? YOU ARE FLOODING YOUR OWN HOMES.'

The workers milling around the robot look anxiously at one another, but she urges them on, shouting and waving her arms.

Grot, still ranting at them angrily, brandishes his enormous spanner and starts to roll up his sleeves.

There was no filthy word which he did not chuck in the face of the mob. The dirtiest term of revilement was not dirty enough for him to apply to the mob.

The floor of the power house is now a great sea of milling workers. More of them are still streaming down the steps in the background. Grot's bulky silhouette is seen in back view as he continues to shout and gesticulate at them.

The mob turned red eyes upon him. The mob glared at him ... The man there, in front of them, was abusing them in the name of the machine.

The workers spread out in a long line, shouting and waving their fists. Their women are in the foreground, waving their arms and shouting insults at Grot off-screen.

The robot shouts, throwing her hands in the air, and the milling workers around her surge forward waving their fists.

For them, the man and the machine melted into one. Man and machine deserved the same hatred. They pushed forward against man and machine.

The workers surge towards Grot in the foreground. He hits one of them with his spanner, picks up another bodily and throws him back into the crowd, but still they come on.

Reverse shot of Grot in front of the control panel. The workers move towards him, lifting him bodily into the air as he fights and struggles.

'Death!' yelled the victorious mob. 'Death to the machines!' yelled the victorious mob. They did not see that they no longer had a leader. They did not see that the girl was missing from the procession.

The robot rushes up to the large switch which controls the power level; on the wall beside it is one of the big thermometers we have seen previously. She looks from side to side with an evil gleam in her eye, then throws the switch ...

Behind her the machine began to race ...

Seen from below, the vast drum of the main generator revolves slowly. Then suddenly lights begin to arc and flash around its circumference.

Meanwhile, more and more workers continue to pour down into the power house.

The robot glances evilly from side to side. A pointer on the wall above her has swung right off the scale.

The heart of Metropolis, John Fredersen's city, began to run up a temperature, seized by a deadly illness . . .

The front line of the workers is seen from a low angle, shouting and ranting. They gaze up at the generator off-screen and grin and cry out in triumph . . .

While on the generator the contacts arc whiter and whiter, and great jagged streaks of lightning flicker across the drum.

The workers gaze up at the spectacle, shouting and laughing in maniac glee . . .

While the generator flashes whiter and whiter still.

We look over the mob of workers, milling across the floor and up the steps.

They all shout joyfully, waving their fists in the air.

The robot is meanwhile still standing by the giant thermometer on the wall. Suddenly it begins to rise rapidly towards danger point. She runs off.

We now seen an iron ladder running up the side of the power house. The robot's shadow is projected on the wall as she rushes up the ladder, glances behind her and backs into a doorway.

Long shot of the vast generator with the control panel beneath it. Lights continue to flash on the revolving drum and great arcs sprout from the vast coils on either side.

> *The power, which was still increasing, now gathered itself together and, hissing, sent out snakes, green, hissing snakes, in all directions.*

The robot runs through the doorway at the top of the ladder and shuts the door behind her.

TITLE : AT LAST MARIA MANAGED TO ESCAPE.

The scene changes to the exterior of Rotwang's house, squatting in the gloom of the city. Night has fallen, and there are lights shining in the cliff-like blocks beyond. Suddenly the front door is flung open, letting out a stream of light. The real Maria appears in the doorway and pelts rapidly towards us, going off at the bottom of frame.

Seen in back view, she arrives at an empty cage standing in one of the passenger lift shafts. There are glowing indicators on the wall on either side. She checks where the other lifts have stopped, then hurries into the cage and operates the controls. The barrier at the front rises up and the lift begins to descend slowly out of sight. We resume on a long shot of the generator in the main power house. It is mounted on a great concrete plinth with a flight of steps leading up to the control panel at the bottom. A body lies on the floor at the bottom of the steps, while great electric arcs shoot out from the generator, reaching right across the room.

Meanwhile, in a cavernous pump room beneath the workers' city, water is flooding up, fountaining into the air.

On the generator, the arcing electricity reaches out and plays along the railings at its foot, while the drum revolves slower and slower.

> *Then, from their glittering thrones, Baal and Moloch, Huitzilopochtli and Durgha arose. All the god-machines got up, stretching their limbs in a fearful liberty. Hungry fires smouldered up from the bellies of Baal and Moloch, licking out of their jaws.*

The great machine room is empty of people. Lights flash everywhere and suddenly great clouds of smoke rise in the centre of the shot.

Back on the generator, the flickering bolts of lightning start to reach down the steps.

Meanwhile, down in the workers' city, the lift cage carrying the real Maria descends slowly into view.

Seen in medium close-up, Maria hurries forward and looks over the edge of the descending lift-cage.

With her, we look down into the city square with the great gong in the centre. It is completely deserted.

In the machine room seen earlier, gouts of steam spout from all sides, filling the picture.

In the power house, the brilliant arcing dies away. The great drum of the generator topples and a debris of smashed girders and masonry begins to fall from the ceiling.

Down in the workers' city, Maria runs out of the lift towards us, looking round wildly.

Behind her, a lift cage suddenly comes shooting down one of the shafts and crashes to the ground, exploding in a great cloud of smoke.

Maria whips round at the noise. Camera tracks in as she starts forward in terror, clapping her hands over her ears and staring up at the spectacle off-screen.

We now see three of the lift shafts in a row. There is an explosion, and clouds of smoke arise from the lift she has just come out of.

She gasps, staring in horror . . .

While smoke and steam billow from the central lift and a fierce light glows from the bottom.

She starts forward, seen from above, while the glow from the conflagration shines on her, almost obscuring her from view.

In long shot, she hurries towards the blazing shaft, then halts.

Then in close-up again she clasps her hands to her mouth and looks up at something off-screen . . .

As the cage in the next lift shaft comes crashing down and explodes. In front of it, Maria staggers back, almost engulfed in the smoke.

She turns and looks off in horror towards the other side . . .

As another lift cage crashes to the ground and great clouds of smoke fill the screen.

Another cage falls.

Maria is seen in close-up, shuddering in horror at the spectacle. She turns, then gasps as her eye falls on something else, beneath her.

Like a dark, crawling beast, in no hurry, the water wound its way across the smooth street.

In the square, black muddy water is beginning to ooze from a crack in the concrete. The flow grows bigger, then suddenly the water starts to gush out in a great stream.

Seen from below, Maria starts back with horror in her eyes, pointing helplessly . . .

As a great geyser of water suddenly fountains up in a street between the tenement blocks.

In the pump room beneath the city, water is spurting out from the shattered casings of the pumps.

In another street, water floods round a corner in the background and comes towards us in a great tide.

Maria dashes into view along another street. She halts and looks off-screen.

At the entrance to one of the tenement blocks, water is gushing down the steps into the street. A child comes hurrying down the steps, looking anxiously behind it.

Maria runs forward, going off in the foreground . . .

Then is seen from behind as she rushes up and picks up the child, who has stumbled on the steps amid the gushing water. More children come pelting down the staircase in the background and they all rush off.

We look down on the great square of the workers' city with the gong on its plinth in the centre. Maria appears from the left, deposits the child at the foot of the plinth and moves towards the gong.

The child follows her as she scrambles up to the levers which operate the mechanical beater for the gong.

Seen from the side she struggles to pull the lever back . . .

And more children run up as she finds that it is too stiff for her. Seen from above, she finally manages to wrench the lever across and the great beater starts to bang against the gong in the foreground.

We look across to a street corner as children of all ages begin to rush out of the lighted doorways of the tenement blocks and stream across to the left.

High angle shot of the children running, bare-footed. They disappear and a couple of seconds later the sinister black flood of

108

water comes after them.

They came, stumbling and crying, coming in troops, ghastly spectres, like children of stone, passionlessly begotten and grudgingly born. They were like little corpses in mean little shrouds, aroused to wakefulness on Doomsday by the voice of the angel, rising from out rent-open graves. They clustered themselves around Maria, screaming because the water, the cool water, was licking at their feet.

Seen from above the water is gushing into the square from all directions, while in the centre the children rush up and crowd round the plinth. They reach up towards Maria, who has let go of the lever and is now trying to force it across again.

A great mountain of water gushes out of the ground, while more hurrying children go past on either side.

We look out from one of the tenement doorways into the water-filled street. The children pelt past in the background, while others come out of the doorway, backs to camera.

Down in the square, more and more children crowd round Maria, who has set the gong beating again.

At a street corner, more children rush out of the tenements and mill around in confusion as the water rises round their ankles.

Resume on Maria at the gong, the children crowding round her. She pulls a second lever.

More children come rushing towards camera. The water is now up to their calves. It suddenly fountains up in the foreground, filling the screen.

By the doorway of one of the tenement blocks, water suddenly gushes out from the wall, hurling the boards carrying the workers' numbers, and pieces of masonry, into the flooded street.

Another shot of the face of the tenement block. Water pours out from beside the doorway while, further up, the wall crumbles under the pressure and great blocks of masonry fall to the ground.

The children struggle through the rising flood, a spray of water shooting across the screen in the foreground.

Camera tracks with a child as it struggles through the water, dragging a little girl by the hand, another child clinging round its neck.

Close-up of another child, soaked, waving its hands in the air as it shouts: *'Help, help!'*

Another shot of spurting water with the hurrying figures of children on every side.

In the centre of the square, Maria leans exhausted against the lever by the beating gong. The children crowd round, stretching out their arms towards her, while water cascades down from one of the tenements in the background.

Seen from above, the children are now up to their chests in water; the beating gong is in the foreground.

From far above, we look down on the children—a little island of humanity in the midst of the flood of water, surmounted by the great white disc of the gong, with Maria leaning exhausted at its side. As we watch, more children run up through the rising waters. The scene changes to a subterranean passage somewhere in the city; water is pouring down across an opening on the left. Freder and Joseph appear at the top of some steps in the background and splash forward along the tunnel. They halt for a moment by the cascade, then Freder waves Joseph on, but he stops, cocking an ear, and beckons to Freder as he hears in the distance . . .

The great round metal beater sounding on the gong—moving towards camera and away again.

The two men listen, then scramble forward through the cascade and off to the left.

Still more children are seen from above, rushing out and along the flooded streets. Water cascades across in the foreground.

In another flooded street, with water fountaining out on every side, Freder runs away from the camera, followed some distance behind by Joseph. He halts in the background and points off to the right, and they both disappear in that direction . . .

While the gong still sounds the alarm, the beater intermittently filling the screen.

Seen from above, Freder pelts forward through the rising flood, white foam splashing out on every side of him.

We look down on a sea of children's faces, hands stretching up hopelessly towards Maria off-screen, calling for deliverance.

A closer shot of the children, jostling one another as they wave.

Maria leans exhausted against the levers, a child helping her as the gong continues to beat. Suddenly Freder scrambles into view behind her. She turns and throws herself into his arms with a gasp. They gaze into each other's eyes, oblivious of their surroundings, and Freder says:

TITLE : 'YES, YOU ARE THE REAL MARIA.'

Down in the flooded square, Joseph stands soaked from head to foot, waving his arms and shouting.

Freder draws away from Maria and looks towards him . . .

While Joseph shouts and gestures, saying:

TITLE : 'TO THE AIR SHAFT—QUICKLY ! THE RESERVOIRS HAVE BURST.'

On top of the plinth, Freder beckons the children across to the left while Maria gathers as many as she can up in her arms.

Several children rush towards Joseph and he lifts one of them up . . .

While Freder and Maria stand by the gong, urging the children on.

Seen from above, the children file past Joseph, who grabs several of them by the hand and hurries them along. A great white fountain of water is gushing out of the flood in the background.

Maria holds a child in her arms, Freder takes another on his shoulders . . .

Then, as water gushes out from every corner of the stricken city, a great column of children advance through the flood towards us with Freder and Maria in their midst.

Water sprays across in front of the camera lens while Joseph beckons the children on.

We now see the metal staircase leading up the air shaft. Joseph appears in the foreground, followed by the children, and points towards it.

Seen from above, the children start to stream up the staircase while the water rises round the base.

Joseph stands surrounded by childen as they surge past him; he shouts and waves them on.

Some way behind, Freder and Maria are struggling through the flood, each carrying a small child. He shouts to her as water sprays across in front of them . . .

While back at the staircase, Joseph beckons frantically, surrounded by surging children.

Far above, in the darkened city of Metropolis, light floods from the cliff-like buildings around the New Tower of Babel; vehicles speed across the overhead ways, searchlights play, lights flash on and off; everything seems normal.

In his office, the Master of Metropolis sits alone at his great curved desk, looking out over the city through the window off-screen. The flashing lights play across the darkened room.

> *The searchlights raved in a delirium of colour upon the windows which ran from floor to ceiling. Cascades of light frothed against the panes. Outside, deep down, at the foot of the New Tower of Babel, boiled the Metropolis.*

We look down on an animated city scene—vehicles moving across overhead tracks, cars and trains racing along at street level, lights shining on every side.

Then we see the ruined generator in the power house, standing in the gloom with broken and twisted girders strewn across it. Electric arcs fountain forth from the control panel, filling the screen in a blaze of white light.

Resume on Fredersen, his chin on his fists as before. He starts, then leans slowly forward as the rhythm of flashing lights seems to change off-screen.

We look down into the city; all the lights flash wildly a few times, then go dim.

Fredersen starts forward from his chair and leans across the desk, then picks up a torch. He turns round, switching it on, and shines the beam across at the double doors leading into his office.

Lit by the circle of light, Slim—the tall dark servant we saw in the Fredersen residence—rushes in through the doorway and pauses with one arm raised.

> *His tall body, with the impression it gave of asceticism and cruelty, the movements of which had, in John Fredersen's service, gradually gained the disinterested accuracy of a machine, seemed quite out of joint, shaken out of control.*

Fredersen shines the torch in Slim's face as the latter rushes forward; then he drops the torch in shock and staggers like a man who has been shot, as Slim hurriedly recounts what is happening below. He falls forward by his desk.

In the workers' city far beneath the surface of Metropolis, all the lights have gone out in the tenements and their walls are crumbling, crashing to the ground. Great fountains of water shoot forth from every side, filling the screen.

Meanwhile Freder and Maria have just reached a landing on the iron staircase in the air shaft. As he is helping her up the last few steps, the structure lurches wildly and they both fall to the ground.

Beneath them, the whole workers' city is crumbling into ruins amid the roaring flood of water.

We look up the next section of staircase. As the children hurry past in the background, Joseph suddenly appears and leans over the stair-rail, calling frantically down to Freder.

On the landing below, Maria is lying slumped against the wall, while Freder staggers to his feet, clutching his head. A light flickers and goes out, off-screen. Freder glances up in alarm, then quickly hauls Maria to her feet.

Joseph is seen from below, shouting frantically. Then he hurries back down the staircase.

We next see the two men coming up the staircase, supporting the exhausted Maria between them. As they pause on a landing, she asks if the children are safe.

In his office, Fredersen sits slumped over his desk with his servant Slim standing stiffly behind him. Fredersen looks round wearily, turns to Slim, then suddenly staggers to his feet.

Lit from below by his torch, Fredersen leans towards Slim and asks:

Title: 'Where is my son?'

Slim is seen from below; he is dressed all in black with curiously pointed ears. He raises a hand and says dramatically:

Title: 'Tomorrow thousands will ask in anguish—"Where is my son"?'

> *His eyes bore an awful hatred. He stood, leaning far forward, as if ready to pounce on John Fredersen, and his hands became claws . . .*

Fredersen stares frantically at Slim, who is seen in back view. He throws up his hands shouting: *'No, no!'*, then claps his hands over his ears and staggers away from him.

We return to the trio on the staircase in the airshaft. In reply to Maria's question, Joseph points to the children off-screen. Maria's

eyes light up. They all stagger forward, camera tracking in front
of them, and the children rush into their arms. Maria turns to
Freder and says:

TITLE : 'SAVE THE CHILDREN—I WILL TELL THE WORKERS THAT
THEY ARE SAFE.'

Joseph nods eagerly in the background as Maria finishes speaking;
she steps towards us and looks around her.

In the main machine room, the Pater Poster machine lies in ruins.
Smoke and steam rise lazily from the shattered remains of the
great steam chests, while in the foreground the workers dance
wildly round in celebration.
By the side of the great ramp at the centre of the machine, Grot
scrambles to his feet, covered in filth, and looks round at the workers
off-screen . . .
As they continue to circle round and round.
Meanwhile, outside the Eternal Gardens, an immaculately dressed
flunkey stands holding aloft a candelabrum, as Joseph and Freder

usher the filthy, ragged children of Metropolis in through the door.
Seen against the shattered remains of one of the great steam
chests, the workers circle round and round in their frantic dance.
Camera pans to show Grot in the background; he hits at them
angrily as they scamper past, trying to break into the circle. Then
he turns and runs half way up the steps on the ramp behind him.
Seen from below, Grot throws up his hands and screams loudly
at the workers. Getting no response, he climbs a few more steps,
turns and tries again.
Close-up of him with bulging eyes; he puts two fingers in his mouth
and gives a great whistle; nothing happens; he tries again.
We now see Grot standing on the steps with his back to us, the
workers circling merrily beneath him. At the sound of his whistle
they stop, breaking the circle, and gaze up at him.
Reverse shot with Grot in the background. The workers crowd
forward to listen. Steam wafts across the great room.
Seen from below, Grot is shouting, swathed in steam.
Resume on the previous shot; as he shouts and waves his arms,
more workers crowd forward in the foreground.
At the bottom of the steps, the workers and their women crowd
forward, shouting up angrily at Grot off-screen . . .
While Grot, his hair flying, gestures wildly and shouts:

Title: 'Where are your children?'

Resume on him as he finishes speaking.
The workers and their women look questioningly at one another,
then shout up to Grot again.
Grot bellows at them, waving his arms:

Title: 'The entire workers' city is under water.'

At the bottom of the steps, the workers fall forward, shouting and
wailing, clawing at their hair in grief.
Grot shouts, beating his chest:

Title: 'Who told you to destroy the machines, you fools—
and thus to destroy yourselves?'

He weeps with rage and sorrow as he speaks.
The workers' women throw back their heads and glare up at him,
waving their arms in a frenzy of grief.

116

In a long shot of the steam-filled room, Grot stands on the steps in the background, the workers milling around in front of him. They wave their fists angrily as he shouts at them.

He is seen from below, against a shattered steam chest, as he shouts:

TITLE: 'THE WITCH! SHE'S TO BLAME FOR ALL THIS. FIND HER! KILL HER!'

Resume on Grot as he finishes.

Seen from above, the workers roar their approval as Grot comes down the steps towards them.

Then in reverse shot they all surge towards camera, leaving behind them the shattered remains of the great Pater Noster machine.

The milling heads of the workers are replaced by those of moving dancers as we move to Yoshiwara, the pleasure-centre of Metropolis. There is a stage in the background; great drapes hang from the ceiling. The gilded youth of Metropolis are dancing wildly, holding Chinese lanterns above their heads. In their centre, the robot, still dressed in the same simple clothes as Maria, is held aloft, circling round and round.

Seated astride the shoulders of a youth in evening dress, she shouts to the assembled company with maniac glee:

TITLE: LET'S WATCH THE WORLD GOING TO THE DEVIL!'

Her bearer turns her on his shoulders, and with her arms flung wide she is carried towards the back of the shot. The bystanders clear a pathway as two men in evening dress precede her up some marble steps and draw back the great drapes to reveal a further flight of steps leading out of the building.

Held aloft on her bearers' shoulders, she pauses at the foot of the second flight of steps and beckons the crowd after her. Then they all turn and surge forward out of the building.

Outside, we look up towards the fantastic ornate entrance to Yoshiwara as the revellers surge down into the street.

The air was a blood red stream, which poured itself forth, flickering, formed by a thousand torches. And the torches were dancing in the hands of the beings who were crowding out of Yoshiwara.

Then we look down on the robot, held aloft, as the crowd circle and dance wildly on every side of her.

And the girl was screaming in Maria's voice: 'Dance—dance —dance! . . .' It seemed as if she were riding on the torches. She raised her knees to her breast, with laughter which brought a moan from the dancers of the procession . . .

With the robot in their centre, the revellers form a glittering, constantly moving procession as they surge towards camera, dancing on through the streets of Metropolis.

Each was dancing the dance of Death with his own torch, whirling madly about, and the whirl of the dancers formed a train, revolving in itself.

Somewhere near Yoshiwara, the cars of the elite of Metropolis stand parked at the foot of a long flight of steps, their headlamps glowing. Suddenly the crowd of workers from the machine room come streaming down the steps towards us with Grot at their head. Seen from above, the workers surge past in a great mass, waving poles, crow-bars, sledge-hammers, weapons of all kinds.

The burly figure of Grot arrives at the bottom of the steps amongst the parked cars. Suddenly, he halts and looks up.

Facing us, he holds the others back, his eyes popping out of his head. They all gaze off-screen in awe at the spectacle which meets their eyes. Then Grot rushes forward and points a trembling finger . . .

Far away, on the other side of the city, the revellers come dancing towards us, the robot circling wildly on her escort's shoulders as she leads them along.

The smoke-swathes from the torches hovered like the grey wings of phantom birds above the dancing train.

Grot stands with the workers behind him, all staring with contorted faces at this vision of evil and corruption. Then they rush forward, filling the screen.

Like a collapsing wall, the mass hurled itself forward, shook itself loose and began to tear along, roaring loudly.

Seen from above, they surge up some more steps towards us, Grot first, the others behind, waving their weapons in the air.

They arrive at the top of the steps and stream towards camera, shouting and throwing their sledge-hammers as they advance.

From a very high angle we look down onto a great viaduct leading between the canyon-like walls of the city buildings. The workers stream across in a long column with the bulky figure of Grot at their head.

At the double opening of the street which led to the cathedral, the stream of dancers from Yoshiwara coincided with the roaring stream of workmen and women.

Seen from above, the revellers come dancing towards us, past the columns of tall buildings. Suddenly the workers converge on them from the left, and surging, milling bodies fill the screen.

Further back, more workers surge past the entrance to the Eternal Gardens, waving their sledge-hammers.

In a high angle shot, Joseph swings open one of the great double doors and looks out into the street, while the workers rush past in the foreground.

We return to the place where the two streams have met. Seen from above, the revellers scatter and the workers all converge on Grot, who has grabbed hold of the robot. After a struggle, he succeeds in pinning her arms behind her back while she laughs with maniac glee. The workers stand round in a circle, shouting, laughing and waving their sledge-hammers.

Joseph stands with his back to us, looking out through the doorway of the Eternal Gardens; more workers are still surging past outside. He glances back inside, then rushes into the building.

The robot is struggling in Grot's grasp, still laughing wildly. The workers and their women stand round in a semi-circle, shouting and whistling their scorn.

Long shot of the great doorway leading into the Eternal Gardens. Joseph hurries out and looks down the street, followed by Freder. They pelt towards camera, going off in the foreground, while a couple of flunkeys run out after them.

The robot laughs crazily, while Grot holds her arms behind her back with one hand, raising his fist in a triumphant gesture. The workers jeer and shout with glee. Grot staggers towards camera with the robot in his grasp.

We look down a long flight of steps in a gloomy street. Freder and Joseph run up to the top of the steps, then after a hasty consultation Joseph races off in the background while Freder pelts down the steps towards us, into shadow.

Freder ran as he had never run. It was not his feet which

119

carried him—it was his wild thoughts . . .

In the square in front of the cathedral of Metropolis, the workers are constructing a vast bonfire around a massive concrete stake. There are shattered cars, their electric lamps still shining, bits of furniture, wood of all kinds.

Three workers stand on the roofs of the cars, egging on the other workers as they mill around bringing things to the pile.

Two of them unravel a long length of cable, grinning down at the others.

In a reverse shot, we look down from the bonfire. The crowd parts as Grot hauls the figure of the robot towards us; she is still laughing wildly, unconcerned by her predicament.

Grot drags the robot up to the pile from the foreground. The workers surge after them waving their sledgehammers . . .

Then he hauls her up onto the roof of one of the wrecked cars, and we see that her hands are tied behind her back. Camera tilts up as the three workers on top of the pile take her from him and haul her towards the stake.

From a very high angle, we look into the street leading to the cathedral precinct. Freder appears at a run.

> *Streets and stairs and streets and at last the cathedral square.*
> *Black in the background, the cathedral, unlighted, the place*
> *before the broad steps swarming with human beings . . .*

The workers stand looking up towards the bonfire, off-screen as Freder rushes up in the background and tries to fight his way through. The workers grab hold of him angrily and he fights to get free.

The robot is now bound securely to the stake in the centre of the pile. She laughs wildly as Grot seizes her by the hair and shakes her, haranguing the crowd below.

We now see the whole scene, with the great bonfire in the background and in front of it, one of the worker's women gleefully waving a flaming torch.

Seen from above, she dances up and down, whirling the torch round and round.

The robot laughs perversely, whipping her head from side to side, while the light from the torch flickers across her face and smoke rises up in the foreground.

The woman tosses the torch onto the bonfire . . .

And the wooden bodywork of the wrecked cars catches fire and begins to burn fiercely. The workers dance jubilantly round.

> *The pyre flamed up in long flames. The men, the women, seized hands and tore round the bonfire, faster, faster and faster, in rings growing ever wider and wider, laughing, screaming with stamping feet.*

Seen from above, they dance from side to side like children, jeering at the robot off-screen.

Then the crowd parts and several workers haul Freder forward, as if they would throw him on the bonfire too.

Flames and smoke are now rising strongly around the robot as she stands bound to the stake; she whips her head from side to side, laughing wildly . . .

While Freder is held by the grinning workers as they watch the spectacle off-screen. Suddenly, Freder starts throwing up his arms and shouting:

TITLE : 'MARIA !'

He struggles wildly, trying to leap forward, but the grinning

121

workers hold him back.

Again we see the robot at the stake, surrounded by flames and smoke . . .

While the workers hold back the struggling Freder, laughing at him gleefully.

> *He struggled like a wild beast, shouting that the veins of his throat were in danger of bursting. Impotent, he threw back his head and saw the sky over Metropolis, pure tender, greenish-blue, for morning would soon follow after this night.*

The scene changes to the doorway of Rotwang's house. The inventor emerges from the darkness inside and staggers towards us, staring glassily, hands outstretched like a sleepwalker. He goes off in the foreground.

We see him again, preceded by his shadow, as he staggers forward beneath the façade of the cathedral. He suddenly turns and stares off-screen . . .

At the flaming pyre beneath the robot, with the workers dancing wildly on every side.

By the doorway leading into the cathedral, Rotwang shrinks back and disappears behind a statue.

Behind another statue on the opposite side of the doorway the real Maria is hiding, watching the workers off-screen. She takes a step forward . . .

And Rotwang, from his hiding place, notices her.

Maria looks out from behind her statue, staring in horror . . .

At the workers dancing wildly round the bonfire, as it blazes up round the robot made in her likeness.

Maria throws up her hands and rushes forward. But at that moment Rotwang hurries across from the foreground and stands over her, holding out his gleaming artificial hand, as he says:

TITLE: 'IF THE MOB SEES YOU, THEY WILL KILL ME FOR HAVING TRICKED THEM.'

Rotwang stands in back view, his hands clawing the air as he advances towards her. She backs away fearfully and finally stumbles backwards through the door into the cathedral. He follows in hot pursuit.

Inside the cathedral, the glow of the bonfire through the great rose window is projected onto the floor. Maria dashes across the shot, pursued by the inventor . . .

Then starts up the staircase leading to the cathedral tower.

Meanwhile, in the square outside, the flames and smoke continue to rise, half obscuring the robot bound to her stake.

Seen from below, she throws back her head and laughs in devilish glee as the flames lick up around her.

Seen from above, Freder is still struggling to get free from the jeering workers . . .

While the robot laughs wildly, tossing her head from side to side. We move to Fredersen's office; the tall figure of Slim looms over the Master of Metropolis as Joseph dashes in and feverishly recounts the happenings at the cathedral. Fredersen listens in great agitation, then turns and rushes off, with Joseph and Slim following behind.

From the centre of the burning pyre, camera looks down through the flames to the workers holding Freder.

A closer shot of them, laughing and jeering; one of them suddenly takes his hand away from Freder's mouth and points up at the

robot off-screen.

We see the robot at the stake, still moving her head from side to side, laughing wildly. Flames and smoke rise up in the foreground, obscuring her from view. Then as they clear, we see that she is changing back into the metal figure constructed by Rotwang.

The workers all turn and stare upwards in amazement at the figure on the bonfire. They shout and scream, the women sinking to their knees, clapping their hands over their ears and eyes.

Seen in long shot, the workers scatter from the gleaming figure at the stake, and race past camera.

The workers holding Freder let go of him and stare up in horror, shouting:

Title : 'The witch, the witch!'

We look up at the gleaming figure amid the flames and smoke.

A reverse shot shows Freder standing in front of the workers. Suddenly he starts back and points upwards. They all look in the same direction.

Beneath the lower edge of the cathedral's pitched roof is a crumbling parapet. The real Maria races along behind it, pursued by Rotwang.

In the square below, Freder dashes forward with a wild cry . . .

He races up the cathedral steps and in through the doorway . . .

And across the interior of the cathedral towards the belfry stairs. We resume on the parapet, with its sculptured gargoyles looking down over the edge. Maria dashes past camera, pursued by Rotwang . . .

As Freder reaches the bottom of the belfry stairs.

On the parapet, Rotwang finally catches Maria; he grapples with her, she fights him off fiercely . . .

While Freder runs headlong up the steps towards the roof.

Maria struggles fiercely with the inventor, the crumbling parapet in the foreground.

Freder dashes round the corner of the parapet and off again.

Rotwang suddenly glances up, sees Freder approaching off-screen and hurls Maria to the ground behind him.

Link on the motion as she falls to the ground.

Resume on the previous shot. Rotwang stands with arms outstretched, waiting, as Freder rushes up and hits him.

The two men circle round one another, searching for an advantage. They grapple with one another, and Rotwang slowly forces Freder towards the edge of the parapet.

The crumbling balustrade is seen from below as the inventor forces Freder backwards across it, his artificial hand round his opponent's throat. Freder struggles wildly, beating at Rotwang with his fists.

All eyes were turned upwards, towards the heights of the cathedral, the roof of which sparkled in the morning sunshine.

Several workers look up in horror; a woman claps her hand to her head and screams.

Then we resume on the two men fighting, just beside one of the gargoyles on the balustrade.

More workers lean forward, watching in agitation. They suddenly part as Fredersen rushes towards camera, halts, and stares up at the scene above. Joseph and Slim come up behind him.

Upon the heights of the cathedral roof, entwined about each other, clawed to each other, wrestled Freder and Rotwang, gleaming in the sunlight.

Seen from below, Freder beats off Rotwang, who is gripping his neck with his artificial hand.

The slender form of the boy, in white silken tatters, bent under the throttling grip of the great inventor, farther and farther backwards.

In the square below, Fredersen slowly raises his hands to his head in horror; Joseph and Slim stand on either side in the background. Resume on the parapet. The two men have come round to the other side of the gargoyle, where the balustrade is even more broken away. The statue's arm shatters and falls as they fight.

Down below, Fredersen falls to his knees, his hands clasped to his forehead.

Back to the two men fighting; they circle round the gap in the parapet . . .

While the workers begin to crowd forward, round the kneeling figure of the Master of Metropolis, jeering and pointing. Angrily, Joseph and Slim thrust them back.

Seen from above, the workers start forward, waving their fists and shouting:

TITLE: 'WHERE ARE OUR CHILDREN?'

John Fredersen heard nothing . . . Only his eyes remained alive. His eyes, which seemed to be lidless, clung to the roof of the cathedral.

We see him in medium close-up, a jeering woman behind him.

Seen from above, Grot steps towards Fredersen off-screen, his eyes bulging, unnoticed by Joseph, who is fighting off the other workers just behind him.

We look down on the scene as the workers lean forward, shouting and taunting Fredersen; on the left, Joseph now pushes back the struggling Grot, who points angrily at Fredersen over his shoulder. The two men struggle fiercely, while the workers fight and jeer in the background. Joseph finally seizes Grot by the lapels and shouts:

TITLE: 'JOHN FREDERSEN'S SON HAS SAVED YOUR CHILDREN.'

The workers crowd forward behind them, disbelieving. Grot shakes Joseph by the shoulders, then, finally convinced, looks round for Freder. Suddenly they all remember where he is and look up in horror at the roof.

Fredersen does likewise. His hands still clasped to his head, his face lit by the glow of the dying bonfire, he mutters :

Title : 'Save my son !'

We return to the two men grappling on the cathedral roof. Freder's shirt is in ribbons; Rotwang has him round the neck and is trying to throttle him. He breaks free, but Rotwang punches him with his artificial hand. Freder staggers back . . .
And lands just by the edge of the crumbling balustrade. He writhes in agony, tries vainly to get up several times, then looks up, stares in horror and finally springs to his feet.

> *Close to the spire a ladder led upwards to the cathedral coping. With the bestial snarl of one unjustly pursued, Rotwang climbed up the ladder, dragging the girl with him, in his arms.*

We see the inventor from below as he climbs up the steeply pitched roof, Maria's inert body slung over his shoulder.
Freder springs to his feet with an anguished cry . . .
Rushes to the foot of the iron ladder and clambers up it.
We look down into the square far below, where the white, up-turned faces of the workers are lit by the flickering glow of the

bonfire. Fredersen kneels in their midst, his hands still clutched to his head. They all move agitatedly.

With Maria slung over his shoulder, Rotwang has now almost reached the top-most pinnacle of the cathedral roof.

> *He held her in his ironlike arms, as prey which, now, nothing and no one could tear away from him.*

Beneath them, Freder rushes up the ladder in pursuit.

> *He climbed up the ladder almost at a run, with the blindly certain speed born of fear for his beloved.*

Rotwang runs along a narrow catwalk attached to the ridge at the top. Seeing Freder coming after him, he drops Maria . . .

She hangs precariously, gripping one of the stanchions of the catwalk, writhing in terror as she tries to stop herself sliding into the void below.

Seen from below, Freder has now reached the catwalk. He grapples with Rotwang, while Maria vainly tries to pull herself up again on the left.

The watchers in the square start forward, horror-struck . . .

As the inventor forces Freder back until they are both lying on the catwalk. Suddenly, they topple over the edge and shoot down the sloping roof, out of sight.

> *The yell of fear from the multitude came shrieking up from the depths.*

They land on the parapet and, clasped tightly together, roll over and over towards the gap in the balustrade. Rotwang gets up first and staggers back; Freder raises a leg and trips him.

Standing amid the watchers in the square, Slim clutches his throat in horror.

> *Rotwang saw above him, sharp against the blue of the sky, the gargoyle of a water spout. It grinned in his face. The long tongue leered mockingly at him . . .*

Seen from below, the dark figure of Rotwang staggers back through the gap in the balustrade and shoots down into the void below.

Resume on the watchers in the square. The workers start to run off towards the fallen body.

Seen from above, they surge round the motionless figures of Fredersen and his two companions.

We resume on the three men as the last workers disappear from

view. Still on his knees, hands clasped to his head, Fredersen
looks up to the roof and murmurs :

TITLE : 'THANK HEAVEN !'

> *And those near enough to him heard the weeping which
> welled up from his heart, as water from a rock.*

One after the other, he slowly removes his hands from his head
and drops them to his side. His head falls forward and we see
that his hair has turned completely white. Then he looks up again
and reaches for the helping hand of Joseph, just behind him.

At the bottom of the ladder on the cathedral roof, Freder helps
Maria down onto the parapet. He strokes her comfortably, mur-
muring soothing words as she stands in his arms.

In the square below, Joseph and Slim help Fredersen to his feet.
The Master of Metropolis suddenly dashes off in the foreground.
Joseph makes as if to follow, but Slim holds him back.

A low angle long shot shows the great doorway to the cathedral
with the steps leading up to it. Fredersen rushes into view from
the foreground and disappears into the darkened doorway.

Inside the cathedral, Maria and Freder stand clasped in each
other's arms. He speaks to her tenderly, then kisses her.

We resume on the cathedral entrance—a long flight of steps
leading up to the great arched doorway. We hold on the scene for
some time, then a great column of workers appear from the foreground with Grot at their head and march steadily up the stairs.

A closer shot of the top of the steps. Grot appears at the head of
the workers and suddenly holds out his arms, halting them, as
the figures of Maria, Fredersen and Freder appear through the
doorway in the background. Grot strides forward on his own and
stands confronting Fredersen. Beyond him, Freder whispers something in his father's ear.

We now see the trio at the cathedral door. Maria and Freder stand
watching while the Master of Metropolis takes a step forward and
hesitates, looking off at Grot.

Seen over the heads of the workers at the top of the steps, the
foreman hesitates also, takes a few strides forward and halts again
a few yards away from the other three.

Fredersen makes as if to step forward, hesitates, half lifts his
hand . . .

While Grot shifts from one foot to the other, obviously in a state of great emotion. He raises his hand in a gesture of friendship . . . While Fredersen stands hesitantly, then takes another step forward, Maria and Freder watching anxiously behind.

Freder is seen in medium close-up, watching tensely. He turns as Maria leans towards him tenderly and says:

TITLE: 'THERE CAN BE NO UNDERSTANDING BETWEEN THE HANDS AND THE BRAIN UNLESS THE HEART ACTS AS MEDIATOR.'

Freder nods; his eyes light up, and he starts forward . . .

Grot and Fredersen stand confronting one another in the cathedral doorway. Grot has put his hands in his pockets. Freder comes forward, and speaks urgently, persuasively, in friendly tones. He takes his father's hand in one of his and stretches out his other arm. Grot shifts uneasily from one foot to the other, pulls his clenched fists out of his pockets, finally stretches out a hand. Freder draws the two men together and links their hands. And they stand, gazing solemnly at one another, the foreman and the Master of Metropolis —and between them the white-clad figure of his son.

For the knowledge had come upon them that it was day, that the invulnerable transformation of darkness into light was becoming consummate, in its greatness, in its kindliness, over the world.